I0813561

Bente Presterud

HANDKNITS FROM RAUMA, NORWAY

30 New Takes on Traditional Scandinavian Designs

Trafalgar Square
North Pomfret, Vermont

First published in the United States of America
in 2021 by
Trafalgar Square Books
North Pomfret, Vermont 05053

Originally published in Norwegian as *Hverdagsstrikk i kortreist ull.*

The instructions and material lists in this book were carefully reviewed by the author and editor; however, accuracy cannot be guaranteed. The author and publisher cannot be held liable for errors.

ISBN: 978-1-64601-103-2
Library of Congress Control Number: 2021943946

Interior Design and Layout: Bente C. Bergen
Photo on page 81: Pudder Agency / Julie Pike
Illustration Photos: Adobe Stock
Translation into English: Carol Huebscher Rhoades

Printed in China
10 9 8 7 6 5 4 3 2 1

Table of Contents

HANDKNITS FROM RAUMA

EVERYDAY KNITTING

The "everyday" experiences of life encompass so much—that's just how it is. Some days are gray and tiring, and others glow in bright colors and feel a little livelier; either way, it depends in part on how we look at it, and how we ourselves make choices as we go. For many of us, the days are happier and more colorful in the company of yarn and knitting needles. I've read often enough that there are many good reasons to knit. It's good for your senses, night sleep, and coordination; it reduces stress, staves off dementia, heals pain, helps with depression, and increases creativity and confidence.

But I don't know anyone who actually knits for better vision, or to sleep better at night, or to reduce stress. We knit because we LOVE to knit. Because we just have to do it! It adds color, coziness, comfy pleasure, and happiness to our lives. So we fill every day with knitting needles and soft skeins of yarn to transform into lovely handknit garments we can wear and share.

LOCAL—TOTALLY NORWEGIAN, TOTALLY GENUINE

This book is filled with garments knitted in local wool—which is to say local for me, here in Norway. Everyone knows that sheep are delightful animals in general, and I love to talk about the characteristics of wool from good Norwegian sheep. Perhaps, right now, some are grazing in a meadow outside a friend's kitchen window, or perhaps there are some black sheep on a large farm in a nearby neighborhood.

The wool I used in these patterns is blended, carded, spun, plied, skeined, dyed, and wound into balls on Veblungsnes in Romdalen—where Rauma Wool Mill does everything needed to transform wool into yarn. For me, it's local and environmentally-friendly yarn. For you, "Norwegian" may not mean "local." Even if you choose to stick with Rauma yarns for these designs, consider checking out yarns and yarn producers in your own local area for your next project!

WOOL IS GOLD

In Norway, we have an especially good eye for wool! It's common here, and Norwegian wool production surpasses baseline sustainability standards when it comes to minimizing environmental damage, from the beginning of the entire production cycle to the final product. The finished yarn is light and lofty, and the garments you knit with it will be warm and durable, and will soften in the wash.

Additionally, all wool, Norwegian or not, has excellent inherent characteristics as a fiber. It is 100% renewable and natural, can hold moisture without feeling wet, wicks moisture away from your skin, retains warmth, and, if it is wet, regulates both cold and heat. It is flame- and bacteria-resistant, and its self-cleaning qualities make garment maintenance easy. Wool doesn't need to be washed often, and wool clothing can just be aired out instead of going into the wash.

BOOK

For all these reasons, I felt there needed to be a book with knitting from Rauma, based on Rauma Garn designs, done in Rauma wool. Because we love to knit. Because it gives our everyday lives color. Because Norwegian sheep are terrific, and their wool is unique.

All the patterns in this book are worked with Rauma yarn, and based on patterns from Rauma Garn designers. The garments are knitted with local-to-me Norwegian wool. I've divided the projects into various groups—and for each group, I dove deep into the archives of Rauma Garn's classics, and found a little treasure to share with you.

I hope you like what you see.

I hope you will be inspired.

I hope every day suddenly becomes a little more colorful, and your knitting needles are itching to knit.

So, enough said. Let's use our time for something more important. Bring out your yarn and needles!

Characteristically Norwegian?

I think of waffles with brown cheese, going out on a hike; never disagreeable, and born with skis on your feet, where no one would believe that anyone could live. Characteristically Norwegian, right?

For me, knitted garments also belong on this list. "Norwegian knitting" is an established and well-recognized concept all around the world. The authentic Norwegian knitted sweater or pullover can even have a distinct look. But most importantly, Norwegian knitting is always comfortable and good, and at-home cozy. It often walks in quietly. It doesn't shout the loudest. But it's really something to be proud of.

Avens Flower Pullover with Round Yoke

Simple sweaters are steadfast friends who are always there for you—wherever you may be. This is one such sweater. It will happily go on a hike in the forest with you. It won't say no to a day in the office. And if you need something to keep you warm on a slightly chilly summer evening, well, you know where to turn.

Design: Rauma Garn / Britt Kathrine Aasen
Photos: Siren Lauvdal

PROJECT SUMMARY

- A pullover with a round yoke
- Stockinette—with ribbing at lower edges of body, sleeves, and around the neckline
- Worked from the bottom up
- Body and sleeves worked separately up to underarms; then all the pieces are placed on the same circular and the yoke is knitted in the round
- Raised back neck

SKILL LEVEL

Experienced

SIZES

XS (S, M, L, XL, XXL)

FINISHED MEASUREMENTS

Chest: 35 (37½, 40¼, 43, 46, 49¼) in / 89 (95, 102, 109, 117, 125) cm

Total Length: 23¼ (24, 24¾, 25½, 26½, 27¼) in / 59 (61, 63, 65, 67, 69) cm

Sleeve Length: from underarm down, 17¾ (18¼, 18½, 18½, 19, 19) in / 45 (46, 47, 47, 48, 48) cm

MATERIALS

Yarn: CYCA #2 (sport, baby) Rauma Finull (100% Norwegian wool, 191 yd/175 m / 50 g)

Yarn Colors and Amounts:

Blue 4124 or Light Yellow Heather 4134: 350 (400, 400, 450, 450, 500) g

Light Blue Heather 4139 or Green Heather 4130: 100 (100, 100, 100, 100, 150) g

Needles: U. S. sizes 1.5 and 2.5 / 2.5 and 3 mm: circulars and sets of 5 dpn

GAUGE

26 sts in stockinette on larger needles = 4 in / 10 cm in width.

Adjust needle sizes to obtain correct gauge if necessary.

BODY

With Blue or Light Yellow and smaller circular, CO 232 (248, 264, 284, 304, 324) sts. Join, being careful not to twist cast-on row; pm for beginning of rnd. Work around in k1, p1 ribbing for 1½ (2, 2, 2½, 2½, 2½) in / 4 (5, 5, 6, 6, 6) cm. Change to larger circular. Pm at side with 116 (124, 132, 142, 152, 162) sts each for front and back. Work around in stockinette until body measures 15½ (16¼, 17, 17¾, 18½, 19¼) in / 39 (41, 43, 45, 47, 49) cm. BO 10 sts centered at each side (= 5 sts on each side of each marker) for underarms. Set body aside while you knit sleeves.

SLEEVES

Make both alike. With Blue or Light Yellow and smaller

dpn, CO 54 (54, 56, 58, 58, 60) sts. Divide sts onto dpn and join; pm for beginning of rnd. Work around in k1, p1 ribbing for 1½ (2, 2, 2½, 2½, 2½) in / 4 (5, 5, 6, 6, 6) cm. Change to larger dpn. Knit 1 rnd, increasing evenly spaced around to 60 (62, 64, 66, 68, 70) sts. Continue in stockinette. *At the same time*, increase 2 sts centered on underarm every 1 (¾, ¾, ¾, ¾, ¾) in / 2.5 (2, 2, 2, 2, 2) cm until you have 88 (96, 100, 104, 108, 112) sts. When sleeve is 17¾ (18¼, 18½, 18½, 19, 19) in / 45 (46, 47, 47, 48, 48) cm long, BO 10 sts centered on underarm.

Pattern A

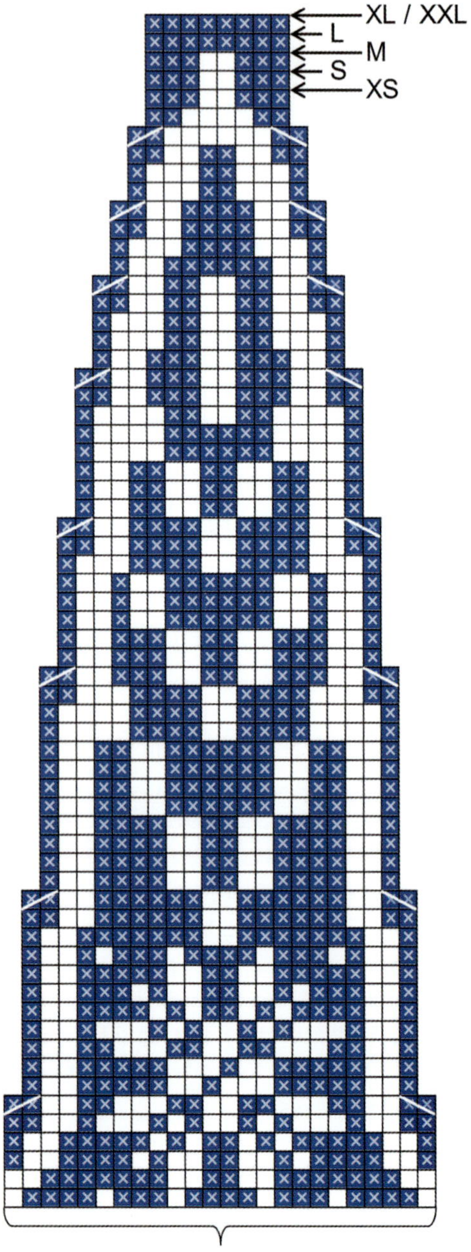

XL / XXL
L
M
S
XS

repeat

YOKE

Arrange body and sleeves on larger circular, matching underarms = 368 (400, 424, 452, 480, 508) sts total. Pm at each intersection of body and sleeve. Work around in stockinette, and *at the same time* decrease 1 st on each side of each marker (= 8 sts decreased on rnd) on every other rnd 4 (5, 5, 5, 6, 6) times = 336 (360, 384, 412, 432, 460) sts rem. On next rnd, decrease 0 (0, 0, 4, 0, 4) sts evenly spaced around = 336 (360, 384, 408, 432, 456) sts rem. Now work following chart for Pattern A, decreasing as indicated on chart. End at the arrow for your size = 112 (120, 128, 136, 144, 152) sts rem. Raise back neck as follows: Knit until 10 sts before center front; turn and purl back until 10 sts before center front. Turn and work 5 fewer sts on each turn. Turn a total of 2 (2, 2, 3, 3, 3) times on each side. For sizes XL and XXL, work another rnd, decreasing evenly spaced around to - (-, -, -, 140, 146) sts.

NECKBAND

Change to smaller circular. Work around in k1, p1 ribbing for 1¼ in / 3 cm. BO loosely.

FINISHING

Seam underarms. Weave in all ends neatly on WS.

- Light Blue Heather or Green Heather
- Blue or Light Yellow Heather
- k2tog
- k2tog tbl

Arches Cardigan for Women and Men

Some cardigans are more cardigan-y than others, I think—and actually I consider this one very close to the Platonic ideal, the ultimate archetype. A two-color, allover pattern, with many panels of various widths and pattern types, and even a hint of Selbu roses.

Design: Rauma Garn / Anne-Kirsti Espenes
Photos: Hilda Kvivik Kavli

PROJECT SUMMARY

- A cardigan with a round neck or V-neck
- Stockinette pattern—with ribbing at lower edges of body, sleeves, on front edges, and around the neckline
- Worked from the bottom up
- The steeked body is knitted in the round to finished length and then cut open for the armholes, neck, and front openings
- The front bands and neckband are worked after the front steek is cut open
- The sleeves are knitted in the round up to the underarms, and then a facing is worked back and forth; the finished sleeves are sewn into the armholes

Women's Round-Neck Cardigan

SKILL LEVEL

Experienced

SIZES

S (M, L, XL, XXL)

FINISHED MEASUREMENTS

Chest: approx. 37¾ (40¼, 42½, 45¼, 47¾) in / 96 (102, 108, 115, 121) cm
Total Length: approx. 24½ (25¼, 26, 26½, 26¾) in / 62 (64, 66, 67, 68) cm
Sleeve Length: approx. 17¾ (18¼, 18½, 19, 19¼) in / 45 (46, 47, 48, 49) cm

MATERIALS

Yarn: CYCA #2 (sport, baby) Rauma Finull (100% Norwegian wool, 191 yd/175 m / 50 g)

Yarn Colors and Amounts:
Natural 401: 300 (300, 350, 350, 400) g
Peasant Blue 438 or Brown Heather 411: 250 (250, 300, 300, 350) g

Needles: U. S. sizes 1.5 and 2.5 / 2.5 and 3 mm: circulars and sets of 5 dpn

Notions: 8-9 buttons

GAUGE

26 sts in stockinette on larger needles = 4 in / 10 cm in width.
Adjust needle sizes to obtain correct gauge if necessary.

BODY

With Natural and smaller circular, CO 271 (287, 303, 319, 335) sts. Work back and forth in k1, p1 ribbing for 4 rows. Place 11 sts at each side on a holder for the front bands = 249 (265, 281, 297, 313) sts rem for body. Change to larger circular. CO 4 new sts for steek (always purl the steek sts; steek sts are not included in stitch counts or pattern). Join and pm for beginning of rnd. Work following chart for Pattern A, and on the last

rnd increase 2 sts evenly spaced around = 251 (267, 283, 299, 315) sts.
Now work the charted patterns in the following order: *Pattern B, Pattern C, Pattern B, Pattern D*; rep * to *, beginning at arrows for your size. Continue as est until body measures 24½ (25¼, 26, 26½, 26¾) in / 62 (64, 66, 67, 68) cm. Set body aside while you knit sleeves.

SLEEVES

Make both alike. Knit in the round.

With Natural and smaller dpn, CO 52 (56, 56, 60, 60) sts. Divide sts onto dpn and join. Work around in k1, p1 ribbing for 4 rnds. On last rnd, increase 1 st. Change to larger dpn. Work Pattern A: count out from center of sleeve to place pattern so it will be centered on sleeve. Work following chart for Pattern A, and on last rnd increase 8 (6, 8, 6, 8) sts evenly spaced around = 61 (63, 65, 67, 69) sts. Shape sleeve by increasing 2 sts centered on underarm on approx. every 5th rnd 23 (24, 25, 26, 27) times = 107 (111, 115, 119, 123) sts.
NOTE: *At the same time*, work in same pattern sequence as for body. Count out from center of sleeve to determine where to begin each chart.
When sleeve is 17¾ (18¼, 18½, 19, 19¼) in / 45 (46, 47, 48, 49) cm long, turn sleeve inside out. With Natural, work 6 rows back and forth in stockinette for facing, increasing 1 st at beginning of each of those 6 rows. BO loosely.

FINISHING

Pm at each side with 125 (133, 141, 149, 157) sts for back and 126 (134, 142, 150, 158) sts for front (do not include the 4 steek sts in count). Pm over the 2 center sts (one on front and one on back) at each side. Machine-stitch 2 lines of fine stitches on each side of center front steek st. Carefully cut steek open up center. Measure sleeve top across width and then measure down body side for armhole depth; pm at base of armhole. Machine-stitch 2 lines of fine stitches on each side of center armhole sts, from shoulder to marker. Carefully cut steek open up center.

FRONT BANDS

Mark neck opening 3¼ (3½, 3½, 3¾, 3¾) in / 8.5 (9, 9, 9.5, 9.5) cm wide on each side of center front and 2¾ (2¾, 2¾, 2¾, 3) in / 7 (7, 7, 7, 7.5) cm deep at center front. Use pins to trace out a smooth, rounded neck opening. Baste along pins. Machine-stitch 2 lines of fine stitches along basting thread. Carefully cut away excess fabric above stitching.

BACK

Mark back neckline as wide as front neck. Make sure the same number of stitches remain for front and back shoulders. Use pins to trace out a smooth, bowed neckline for back, ¾ in / 2 cm deep at center back. Baste along pins. Machine-stitch 2 lines of fine stitches along basting thread. Carefully cut away excess fabric above stitching.
Seam shoulders with three-needle bind-off or mattress stitch.

NECKBAND

Use Natural and smaller circular. Pick up and knit 13 sts for every 2 in / 5 cm all around neck. Work back and forth in k1, p1 ribbing for 2½ in / 6 cm. BO loosely. Fold band doubled to wrong side and sew down.

LEFT FRONT BAND

Use Natural and smaller circular. Place the 11 held sts of one front band onto needle and CO 4 new sts = facing on the side turned towards front edge. Work back and forth with the 11 band sts in k1, p1 ribbing as est and the 4 new sts in stockinette. Continue until band reaches base of neckband when slightly stretched. BO the 4 facing sts. Continue in k1, p1 ribbing to end of neckband. BO in ribbing.
Mark spacing for 8-9 buttons on band. The bottom and top ones are placed about ⅜ in / 1 cm above/below edge and the rest spaced evenly between.

RIGHT FRONT BAND

Work as for left front band but make buttonholes, spaced as for buttons. Buttonhole = BO the 3 center sts of the 11 in ribbing. On next row, CO 3 new sts over gap.

FINISHING

Sew front bands to front edges. Fold facings over cut steek edges and sew down so they are not visible on RS. Attach sleeves, matching center of sleeve tops to shoulder seams. Cover cut armhole edges with facings and sew down facings on WS.
Gently steam press cardigan under a damp pressing cloth.
Sew on buttons.

Pattern A

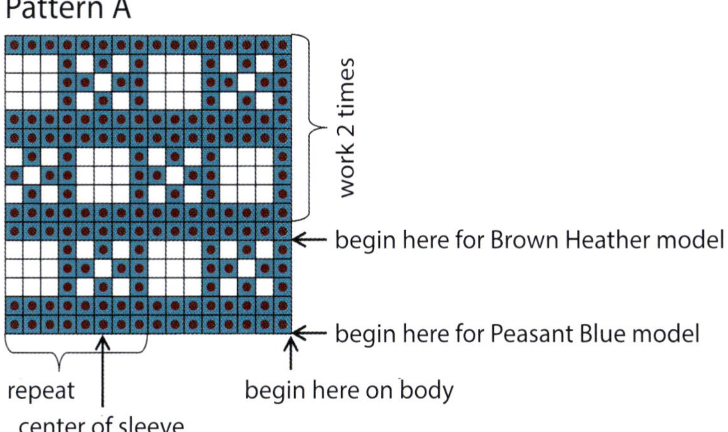

☐ Natural

■ Peasant Blue or Brown Heather

Pattern C

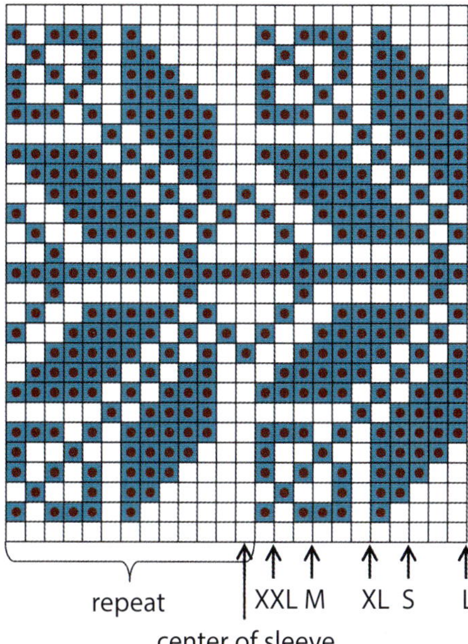

Pattern B

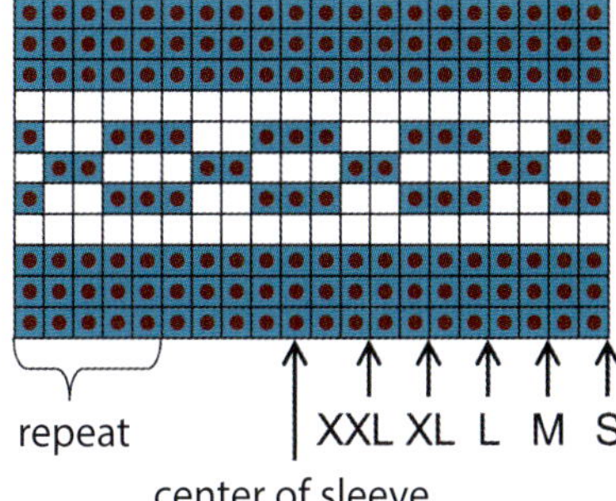

Pattern D

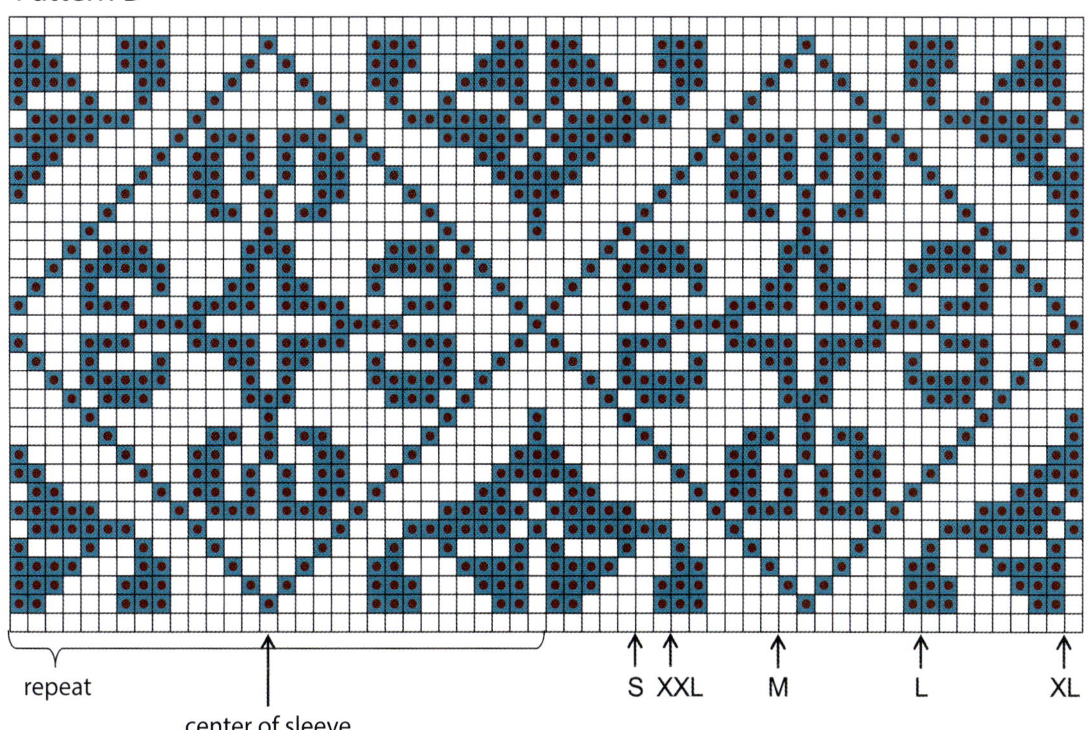

Men's V-Neck Cardigan

SKILL LEVEL

Experienced

SIZES

S (M, L, XL, XXL)

FINISHED MEASUREMENTS

Chest: approx. 40¼ (42½, 45¼, 47¾, 50) in / 102 (108, 115, 121, 127) cm

Total Length: approx. 26 (26¾, 27½, 28, 28¼) in / 66 (68, 70, 71, 72) cm

Sleeve Length: approx. 19 (19¼, 19¾, 20, 20½) in / 48 (49, 50, 51, 52) cm

MATERIALS

Yarn: CYCA #2 (sport, baby) Rauma Finull (100% Norwegian wool, 191 yd/175 m / 50 g)

Yarn Colors and Amounts:

Brown Heather 411 or Peasant Blue 438: 300 (350, 350, 400, 400) g

Natural 401 or Natural 401: 300 (300, 300, 350, 350) g

Needles: U. S. sizes 1.5 and 2.5 / 2.5 and 3 mm: circulars and sets of 5 dpn

Notions: 7-8 buttons

GAUGE

26 sts in stockinette on larger needles = 4 in / 10 cm in width.

Adjust needle sizes to obtain correct gauge if necessary.

EDGING COLOR

Brown Heather cardigan: Brown Heather

Peasant Blue cardigan: Peasant Blue

BODY

With edging color (see above) and smaller circular, CO 287 (303, 319, 335, 351) sts. Work back and forth in k1, p1 ribbing for 4 rows. Place 11 sts at each side on a holder for the front bands = 265 (281, 297, 313, 329) sts rem for body. Change to larger circular. CO 4 new sts for steek (always purl the steek sts; steek sts are not included in stitch counts or pattern). Join and pm for beginning of rnd. Work following chart for Pattern A, and on the last rnd increase 2 sts evenly spaced around = 267 (283, 299, 315, 331) sts.

Now work the charted patterns in the following order: *Pattern B, Pattern C, Pattern B, Pattern D*; rep * to *, beginning at arrows for your size. Continue as est until body measures 26 (26¾, 27½, 28, 28¼) in / 66 (68, 70, 71, 72) cm. Set body aside while you knit sleeves.

SLEEVES

Make both alike. Knit in the round.

With edging color and smaller dpn, CO 56 (60, 60, 64, 64) sts. Divide sts onto dpn and join. Work in k1, p1 ribbing for 4 rnds. On last rnd, increase 1 st. Change to larger dpn. Work Pattern A: count out from center of sleeve to place pattern so it will be centered on sleeve. Work following chart for Pattern A, and on last rnd increase 8 (6, 8, 6, 8) sts evenly spaced around = 65 (67, 69, 71, 73) sts. Shape sleeve by increasing 2 sts centered on underarm on approx. every 5th rnd 24 (25, 26, 27, 28) times = 113 (117, 121, 125, 129) sts.

NOTE: *At the same time*, work in same pattern sequence as for body. Count out from center of sleeve to determine where to begin each chart.

When sleeve is 19 (19¼, 19¾, 20, 20½) in / 48 (49, 50, 51, 52) cm long, turn sleeve inside out. With edging color, work 6 rows back and forth in stockinette for facing, increasing 1 st at beginning of each of the 6 rows. BO loosely.

FINISHING

Pm at each side with 133 (141, 149, 157, 165) sts for back and 134 (142, 150, 158, 166) sts for front (do not include the 4 steek sts). Move sts to two holders (one for front and one for back).

Machine-stitch 2 lines of fine stitches on each side of center front steek st. Carefully cut steek open up center. Measure sleeve top across width and then measure down body side for armhole depth; pm at base of armhole. Machine-stitch 2 lines of fine stitches on each side of center armhole sts, from shoulder to marker. Carefully cut steek open up center.

FRONTS

Mark neck opening 3½ (3½, 3¾, 3¾, 3¾) in / 9 (9, 9.5, 9.5, 9.5) cm wide on each side of center front and 6¾ (7, 7¼, 7½, 7¾) in / 17.5 (18, 18.5, 19, 19.5) cm deep at center front.

Use pins to trace out a smooth, V-neck opening. Baste along pins. Machine-stitch 2 lines of fine stitches along

basting thread. Carefully cut away excess fabric above stitching.

BACK

Mark back neckline as wide as front neck. Make sure the same number of stitches remain for front and back shoulders. Use pins to trace out a smooth, bowed neckline for back, ¾ in / 2 cm deep at center back. Baste along pins. Machine-stitch 2 lines of fine stitches along basting thread. Carefully cut away excess fabric above stitching.

Seam shoulders with three-needle bind-off or mattress stitch.

RIGHT FRONT BAND

Use edging color and smaller circular. Place the 11 held sts of one front band onto needle and CO 4 new sts = facing on the side turned towards front edge. Work back and forth with the 11 band sts in k1, p1 ribbing as est and the 4 new sts in stockinette. Continue as est until band reaches up front edge and all the way to center back neck. Make sure the band doesn't draw in at base of V-neck. BO all sts.
Mark spacing for 7-8 buttons on band. The bottom one is placed about ⅜ in / 1 cm from lower edge and the top one about ⅜ in / 1 cm below base of V-neck, and the rest spaced evenly between.

LEFT FRONT BAND

Work as for right front band but make buttonholes, spaced as for buttons. Buttonhole = BO the 3 center sts of the 11 in ribbing. On next row, CO 3 new sts over gap.

FINISHING

Sew front bands to front edges and along back neck. Fold facings over cut steek edges and sew down so they are not visible on RS.
Attach sleeves, matching center of sleeve tops to shoulder seams. Cover cut armhole edges with facings and sew down on WS.
Gently steam press cardigan under a damp pressing cloth.
Sew on buttons.

Pattern A

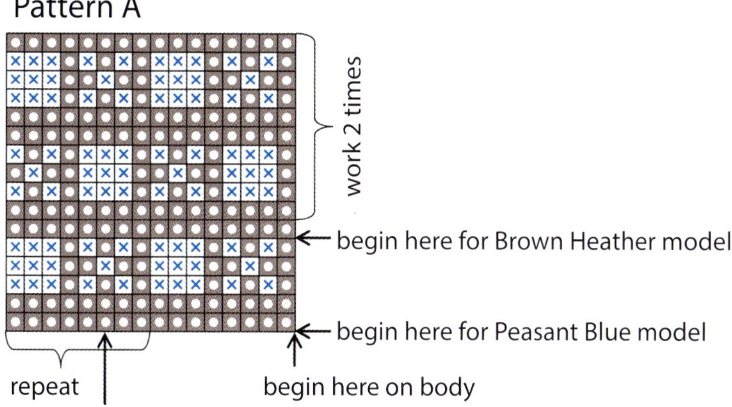

Natural or Peasant Blue

Brown Heather or Natural

Pattern C

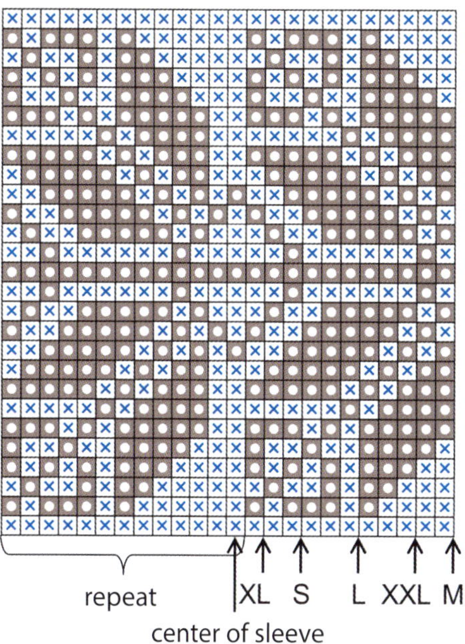

Pattern B

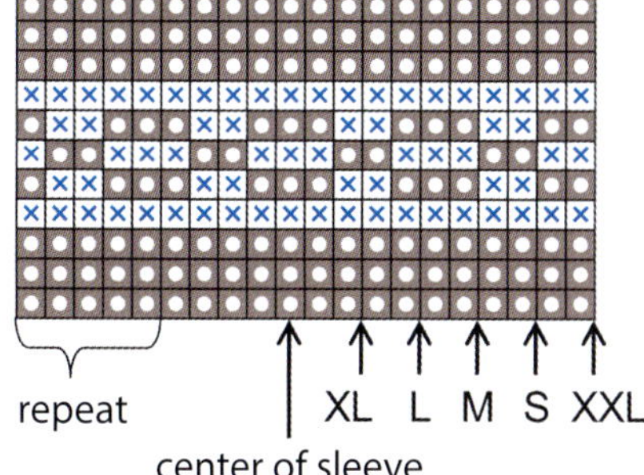

Pattern D

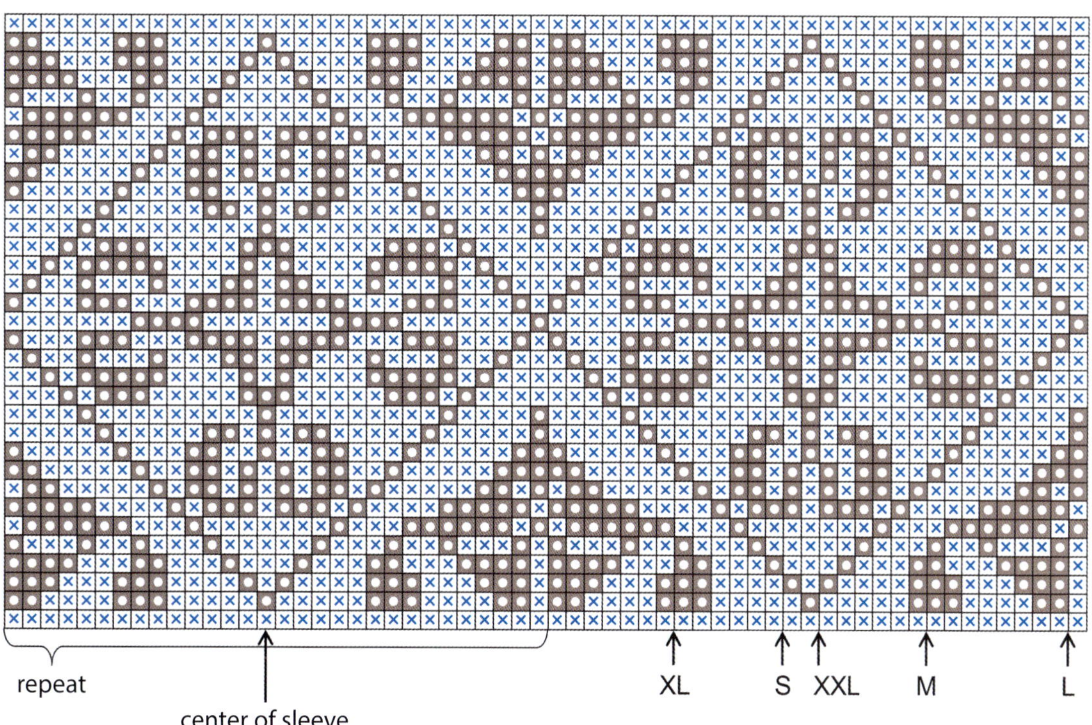

Raglan Pullover with Surprising Panels

At first glance, this pullover seems to be worked with only two colors. I suggest gray and charcoal. However, if you look a bit more closely—whoa, there are three colors. Light gray, brown, and dark blue-gray. Really!

Design: Rauma Garn / Stina Fredriksson
Photos: Siren Lauvdal

PROJECT SUMMARY

- A pullover with raglan shaping
- Stockinette pattern—with ribbing at lower edges of body and sleeves, and around the neckline
- Worked from the bottom up
- The body and sleeves are knitted separately up to the underarms; then all the pieces are placed on one circular and the yoke is knitted in the round
- The sweater has a raised back neck

SKILL LEVEL

Experienced

SIZES

XS (S/M, L, XL, XXL)

FINISHED MEASUREMENTS

Chest: approx. 34¼ (38½, 43, 47¼, 51½) in / 87 (98, 109, 120, 131) cm
Total Length: approx. 24 (24¾, 25½, 26½, 27¼) in / 61 (63, 65, 67, 69) cm
Sleeve Length: approx. 17¾ (17¾, 18¼, 18¼, 18½) in / 45 (45, 46, 46, 47) cm

MATERIALS

Yarn: CYCA # 3 (DK, light worsted) Rauma 3-ply Strikkegarn (100% Norwegian wool, 118 yd/108 m / 50 g)

Yarn Colors and Amounts:
Light Gray Heather 103: 400 (450, 500, 550, 600) g
Dark Blue-Gray 1387: 100 (100, 100, 150, 150) g
Brown Heather 111: 50 (50, 50, 50, 50) g

Needles: U. S. sizes 2.5 and 6 / 3 and 4 mm: circulars and sets of 5 dpn

GAUGE

22 sts and 28 rnds in stockinette pattern on larger needles = 4 x 4 in / 10 x 10 cm.
Adjust needle sizes to obtain correct gauge if necessary.

BODY

With Light Gray Heather and smaller circular, CO 192 (216, 240, 264, 288) sts. Join, being careful not to twist cast-on row. Pm for beginning of rnd and at side = 96 (108, 120, 132, 144) sts each for front and back. Work around in k1, p1 ribbing for 2½ in / 6 cm. Change to larger circular. Work around in stockinette until body measures 10¾ (11, 11½, 11¾, 12¼) in / 27 (28, 29, 30, 31) cm. Work following chart for Pattern A, beginning at arrow for your size. When body measures 15 (15½, 15¾, 16¼, 16½) in / 38 (39, 40, 41, 42) cm, BO 8 sts centered at each side for underarms = 88 (100, 112, 124, 136) sts rem each for front and back. Set body aside while you knit sleeves.

SLEEVES

Make both alike. With Light Gray Heather and smaller dpn, CO 40 (42, 44, 46, 48) sts. Divide sts onto dpn and join. Work around in k1, p1 ribbing for 2½ in / 6 cm. Change to larger dpn. Work around in stockinette. On first rnd, increase 6 sts evenly spaced around = 46 (48, 50, 52, 54) sts. When sleeve is 3¼ in / 8 cm long, begin shaping sleeve by increasing 2 sts centered on underarm on approx. every 1 (¾, ¾, ¾, ¾) in / 2.5 (2, 2, 2, 2) cm 15 (16, 17, 18, 19) times = 76 (80, 84, 88, 92) sts. When sleeve is 13½ (13½, 13¾, 13¾, 14¼) in / 34 (34, 35, 35, 36) cm long, work Pattern B, beginning at arrow for your size. When sleeve measures 17¾ (17¾, 18¼, 18¼, 18½) in / 45 (45, 46, 46, 47) cm, BO 8 sts centered on underarm = 68 (72, 76, 80, 84) sts rem. Make sure you BO at same pattern chart row as on body.

YOKE

Arrange body and sleeves on larger circular, matching underarms = 312 (344, 376, 408, 440) sts total. Pm at each intersection of body and sleeve. Work around in stockinette as est. Shape raglan by decreasing 1 st on each side of each marker as follows: Knit until 2 sts before marker, k2tog tbl, sl m, k2tog = 8 sts decreased on rnd. Decrease the same way on every other rnd a total of 26 (28, 30, 31, 33) times. *At the same time*, after you've decreased 18 (20, 22, 23, 25) times, place 18 (20, 20, 22, 22) sts at center front on a holder for neck. Now work each side separately, back and forth. After completing one side, work opposite side to correspond. Continue to decrease for raglan on every other row (that is, on RS rows). At the same time, shape neck as follows:

Rows 1-2: Sl 1, work until 3 sts rem; turn.

Rows 3-4: Sl 1, work until 5 sts rem; turn.

Continue the same way by working 2 fewer sts each time, until all raglan decreases have been worked. When the neckline meets the raglan line on front, decrease for raglan only on sleeves and back.

NECKBAND

Use smaller circular and Light Gray Heather. Place all neck sts on needle. Knit 1 rnd, adjusting stitch count to 112 (120, 120, 128, 128) sts. Work around in k1, p1 ribbing for 2½ in / 6 cm. BO loosely.

FINISHING

Seam underarms.

Weave in all ends neatly on WS.

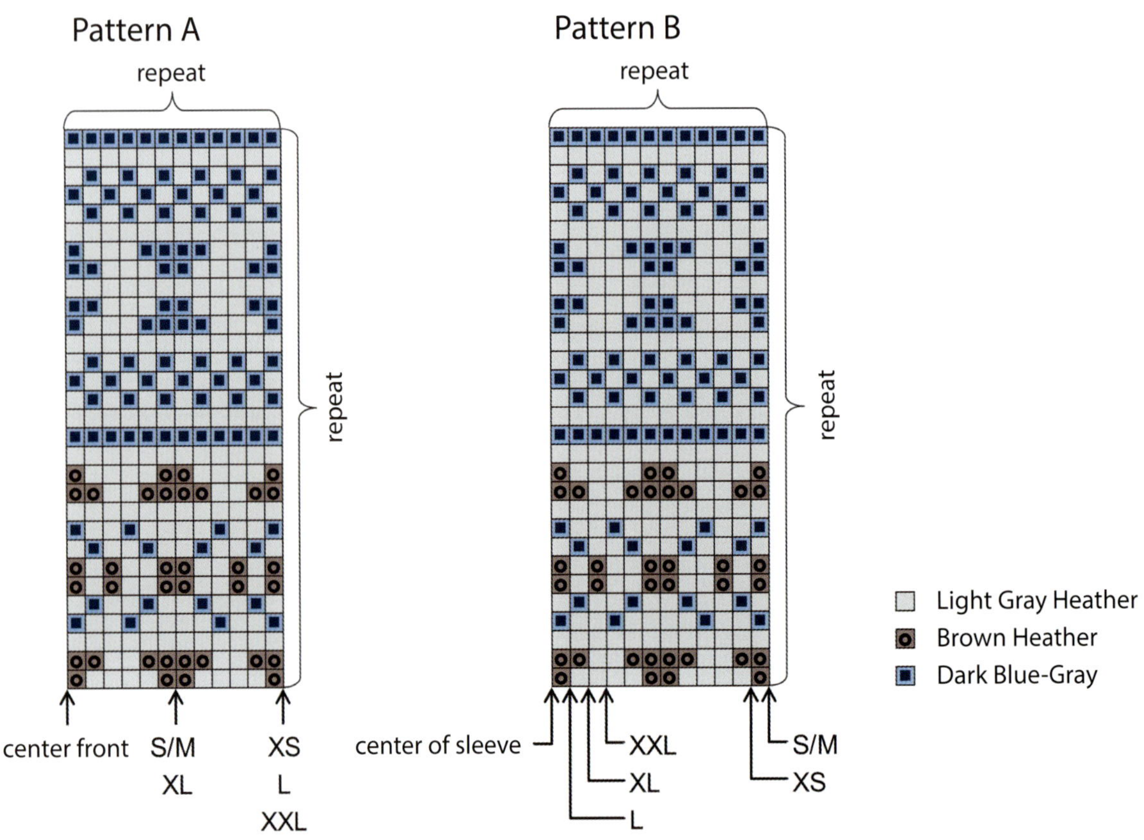

Star Yoke Pullover

Neutral shades are deliciously relaxing. They provide rest and tranquility in our sometimes-dizzying whirligig of daily life. Even so, sometimes a refreshingly eye-catching color play—in orange, for example—is worthwhile, and even vital, almost like a vitamin supplement!

Design: Rauma Garn
Photos: Elisabeth Tollisen

PROJECT SUMMARY

- A pullover with a round yoke
- Stockinette pattern—with ribbing at lower edges of body and sleeves, and around the neckline
- Worked from the bottom up
- The body and sleeves are knitted separately up to the underarms; then all the pieces are placed on one circular and the yoke is knitted in the round

SKILL LEVEL

Intermediate/Experienced

SIZES

XS (S, M, L)

FINISHED MEASUREMENTS

Chest: approx. 32¾ (35, 37½, 40¼) in / 83 (89, 95, 102) cm
Total Length: approx. 22¾ (23¾, 24¾, 25½) in / 58 (60, 63, 65) cm
Sleeve Length: approx. 17¾ (18¼, 19, 19) in / 45 (46, 48, 48) cm

MATERIALS

Yarn: CYCA #2 (sport, baby) Rauma Finull (100% Norwegian wool, 191 yd/175 m / 50 g)

Yarn Colors and Amounts:
Gray 404: 250 (300, 350, 400) g
Natural 401: 100 (100, 150, 150) g
Light Rust-Orange 460: 50 (50, 50, 50) g

Needles: U. S. sizes 1.5 and 2.5 / 2.5 and 3 mm: circulars and sets of 5 dpn

GAUGE

26 sts in stockinette pattern on larger needles = 4 in / 10 cm in width.
Adjust needle sizes to obtain correct gauge if necessary.

BODY

With Natural and smaller circular, CO 216 (232, 248, 264) sts. Join, being careful not to twist cast-on row. Pm for beginning of rnd and at side = 108 (116, 124, 132) sts each for front and back. Work around in k1, p1 ribbing for 1½ (1½, 2, 2) in / 4 (4, 5, 5) cm. Change to larger circular. Work around in stockinette until body measures 2¾ (2¾, 3¼, 3¼) in / 7 (7, 8, 8) cm. Work following chart for Pattern A. After completing charted rows, work around with Gray. When body measures 14½ (15½, 16¼, 17) in / 37 (39, 41, 43) cm, BO 10 sts centered at each side for underarms (= BO 5 sts on each side of each marker) = 98 (106, 114, 122) sts rem each for front and back. Set body aside while you knit sleeves.

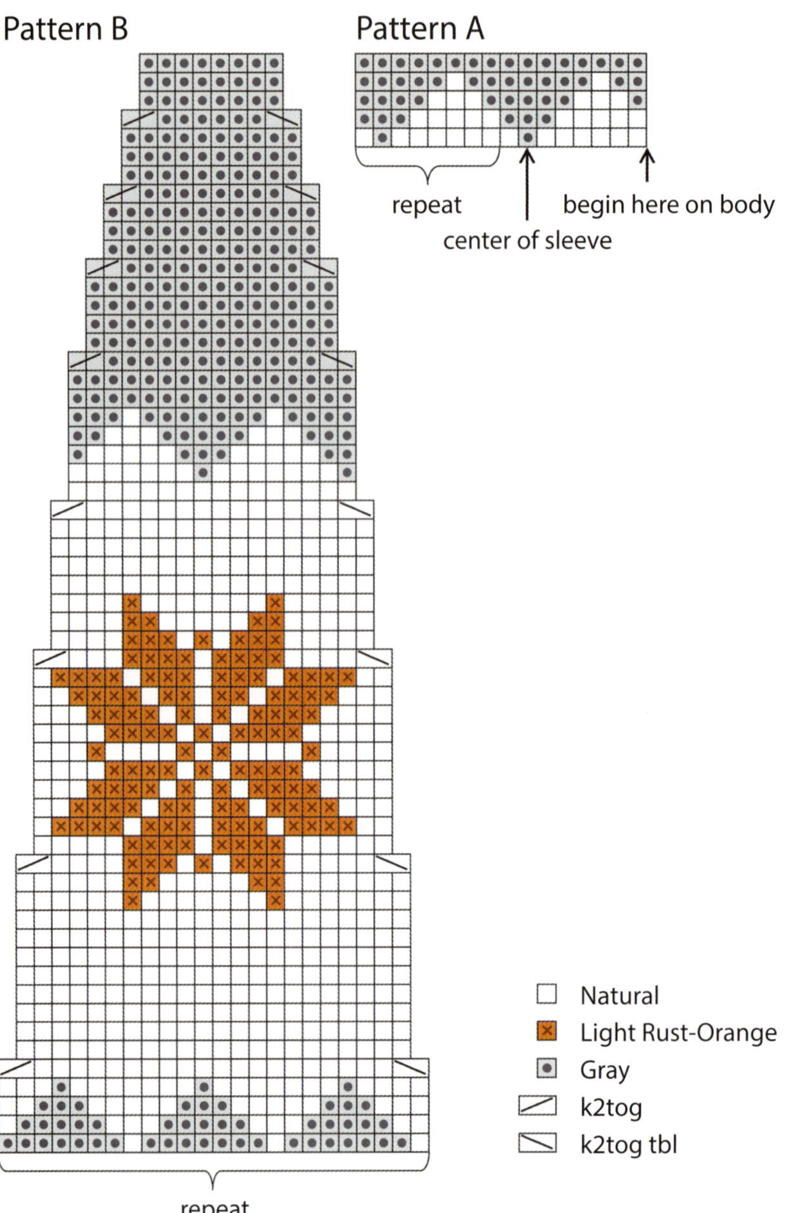
Pattern B
Pattern A
repeat
center of sleeve
begin here on body
repeat
Natural
Light Rust-Orange
Gray
k2tog
k2tog tbl

SLEEVES

Make both alike. With Natural and smaller dpn, CO 52 (54, 54, 56) sts. Divide sts onto dpn and join. Work around in k1, p1 ribbing for 1½ (1½, 2, 2) in / 4 (4, 5, 5) cm. Change to larger dpn. Work around in stockinette until sleeve measures 2¾ (2¾, 3¼, 3¼) in / 7 (7, 8, 8) cm. Work following chart for Pattern A. Count out from center of sleeve to determine where on chart to begin pattern. After completing charted rows, work around with Gray. *At the same time*, begin shaping sleeve by increasing 2 sts centered on underarm on approx. every ⅝ (⅝, ⅝, ⅝) in / 1.5 (1.5, 1.5, 1.5) cm 14 (17, 21, 22) times = 80 (88, 96, 100) sts. When sleeve measures 17¾ (18¼, 19, 19) in / 45 (46, 48, 48) cm, BO 10 sts centered on underarm = 70 (78, 86, 90) sts rem.

YOKE

Arrange body and sleeves on larger circular, matching underarms = 336 (368, 400, 424) sts total. Pm at each intersection of body and sleeve. Work around in stockinette as est. Shape raglan: decrease 1 st on each side of each marker as follows: Knit until 2 sts before marker, k2tog tbl, sl m, k2tog = 8 sts decreased on rnd. Decrease the same way on every other rnd a total of 3 (4, 5, 5) times = 312 (336, 360, 384) sts rem. Now work following chart for Pattern B, decreasing as shown on chart. After completing chart for Pattern B, 104 (112, 120, 128) sts rem.

NECKBAND

Change to smaller circular and, with Light Gray Heather, work around in k1, p1 ribbing for ¾ in / 2 cm. BO loosely.

FINISHING

Seam underarms. Weave in all ends neatly on WS.

Crystal Pullover

If I could be a color, I would be blue! Blue comes in so many wonderful shades, and it's as diverse as both undulating seas and cloudless skies. Or the prettiest crystals, in glittering blue tones!

Design: Rauma Garn / Anne-Kirsti Espenes
Photos: Rauma Garn

PROJECT SUMMARY

- A pullover with a high neck
- Worked from the bottom up
- Stockinette pattern—with ribbing at lower edges of body and sleeves, and around the neckline
- The body is knitted in the round; stitches are bound off for the underarms, and then the front and back are worked separately, back and forth
- Each sleeve is worked in the round to the underarm, and then the sleeve cap is worked back and forth; the sleeves are sewn into the armholes later

SKILL LEVEL

Experienced

SIZES

36 (38, 40, 42, 44)

FINISHED MEASUREMENTS

Chest: approx. 36¼ (38½, 40½, 43¼, 46) in / 92 (98, 103, 110, 117) cm
Total Length: approx. 22 (22¾, 23¾, 24½, 25¼) in / 56 (58, 60, 62, 64) cm
Sleeve Length: approx. 18¼ (18½, 19, 19¼, 19¾) in / 46 (47, 48, 49, 50) cm

MATERIALS

Yarn: CYCA #5 (bulky) Rauma Vams PT3 (100% Norwegian wool, 90 yd/83 m / 50 g)

Yarn Colors and Amounts:
Natural V01: 400 (450, 500, 500, 550) g
Light Denim V50: 100 (100, 150, 150, 150) g
Denim V51: 50 (50, 50, 50, 50) g
Light Turquoise V75: 50 (50, 50, 50, 50) g

Needles: U. S. sizes 6 and 7 / 4 and 4.5 mm: circulars and sets of 5 dpn

GAUGE

18 sts in stockinette pattern on larger needles = 4 in / 10 cm in width.
17 sts in k2, p2 ribbing on smaller needles = 4 in / 10 cm in width.
Adjust needle sizes to obtain correct gauge if necessary.

BODY

With Natural and smaller circular, CO 160 (168, 176, 184, 196) sts. Join, being careful not to twist cast-on row. Pm for beginning of rnd. Work around in k2, p2 ribbing for 2 (2, 2, 2, 2) in / 5 (5, 5, 5, 5) cm. On last rnd, increase 6 (8, 10, 14, 14) sts evenly spaced around = 166 (176, 186, 198, 210) sts. Change to larger circular. Work following chart for Pattern A, beginning and ending at arrows for your size on both front and back. When body measures 13½ (13¾, 14½, 15, 15 ¾) in / 34 (35, 37, 38, 40) cm, work next rnd as follows: BO 3 (3, 4, 4, 5) sts for underarm, k77 (81, 85, 91, 95), BO 6 (7, 8, 8,

10) sts for underarm, k77 (81, 85, 91, 95), BO 3 (4, 4, 4, 5) sts. Begin working front and back separately.

FRONT

Continue in pattern, working back and forth. *At the same time*, shape armholes. At each side, on every other row, decrease 1 st 4 times = 69 (73, 77, 83, 87) sts rem. When piece measures 19¾ (20½, 21¼, 22, 22¾) in / 50 (52, 54, 56, 58) cm, BO the center 15 (15, 17, 17, 19) sts for front neck. Work each side of front separately. Shape neck on every other row: BO 3 sts once, 2 sts once, and 1 st 4 times = 18 (20, 21, 24, 25) sts rem. When piece measures 22 (22¾, 23¾, 24½, 25¼) in / 56 (58, 60, 62, 64) cm, place rem sts on a holder.

BACK

Work as for front, including armhole shaping, until back measures 21¼ (22, 22¾, 23¾, 24½) in / 54 (56, 58, 60, 62) cm. BO the center 27 (27, 29, 29, 31) sts for back neck. Work each side of back separately. Shape neck on every other row: BO 2 sts once, and 1 st 1 time = 18 (20, 21, 24, 25) sts rem. When piece measures 22 (22¾, 23¾, 24½, 25¼) in / 56 (58, 60, 62, 64) cm, place rem sts on a holder.

SLEEVES

Make both alike. With Natural and smaller dpn, CO 40 (40, 44, 44, 48) sts. Divide sts onto dpn and join. Pm for beginning of rnd. Work around in k2, p2 ribbing for 6 rnds. Change to larger dpn and continue in ribbing. When sleeve is 2 in / 5 cm long, begin shaping sleeve: increase 2 sts centered on underarm. Work new sts into ribbing. Increase the same way every 5th rnd a total of 17 (18, 17, 18, 17) times = 74 (76, 78, 80, 82) sts. When sleeve is 18¼ (18½, 19, 19¼, 19¾) in / 46 (47, 48, 49, 50) cm long, BO 8 (8, 8, 10, 10) sts centered on underarm. Continue in ribbing, back and forth. Shape sleeve cap: at each side, on every other row, BO 1 st 4 (5, 6, 6, 7) times and then 8 sts 3 times. BO rem 10 sts.

FINISHING

Seam shoulders with three-needle bind-off or Kitchener st.

NECKBAND

With Natural and smaller short circular, pick up and knit approx. 72 (76, 80, 80, 84) sts around neck—the stitch count must be a multiple of 4. Work around in k2, p2 ribbing for 6¼ (6¾, 7, 7, 7) in / 16 (17, 18, 18, 18) cm. BO loosely in ribbing.

Attach sleeves. Weave in all ends neatly on WS.

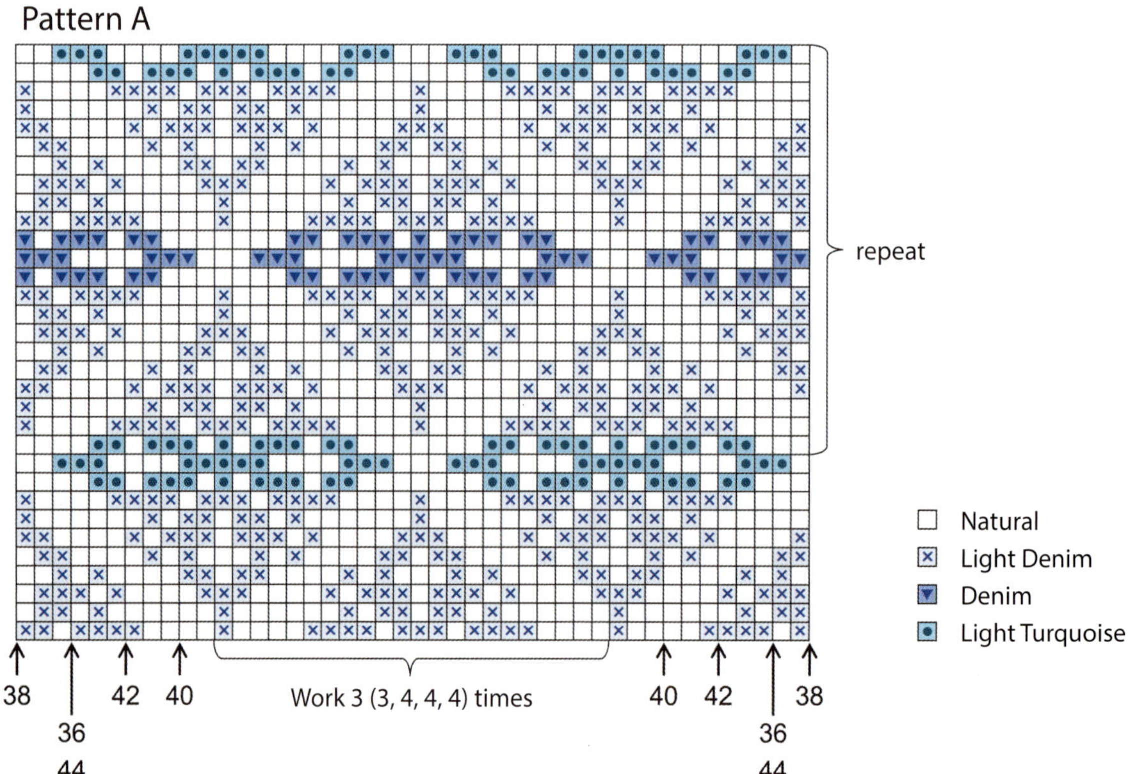

GEMS FROM THE ARCHIVE

Per Spook Pullover

I remember when this pullover pattern was first published—it conquered knitting needles all over the country! It was totally different than anything Norwegian knitters had ever seen before, with a square neck and an unusual use of its motifs. When it was designed by Per Spook in 1981, it could be ordered from the Norwegian Handcraft Association for their 90-year anniversary. The pattern sold around 50,000 copies, and the sweater became a classic. My friend knitted one in gray and white, but the original colors were apparently black and yellow.

(Source: Digitalmuseum.no)

PROJECT SUMMARY

- A pullover that gradually widens from lower edge to underarms
- Square neck
- Stockinette pattern—with facings at lower edge of body; the sleeve cuffs are ribbed
- Worked from the bottom up
- The body is knitted in the round all the way up; the neck begins with stitches bound off across the neckline, and the sweater continues in the round with a steek at center front
- Steeks are later reinforced and cut open for armholes and front neck
- Each sleeve is worked in the round to the armhole, and then a facing is worked back and forth; the sleeves are sewn into the armholes later
- The neck is edged with 2 rounds stockinette

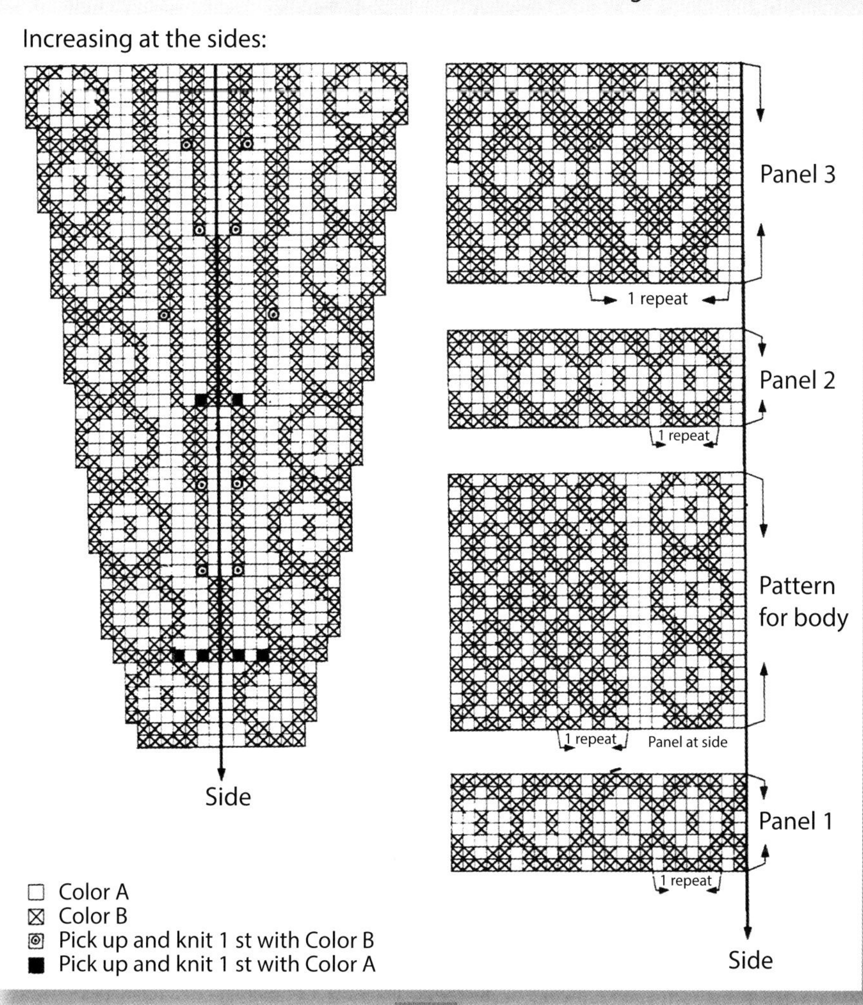

Women's and Men's Pullover

SKILL LEVEL

Experienced

SIZES

Women's 38/40 (Men's 50/52)

FINISHED MEASUREMENTS

Chest: 39½ (47¼) in / 100 (120) cm
Total Length: 25¼ (27½) in / 64 (70) cm
Sleeve Length: 19 (23¾) in / 48 (60) cm

MATERIALS

Yarn: CYCA # 3 (DK, light worsted) Rauma 3-ply Strikkegarn (100% Norwegian wool, 118 yd/108 m / 50 g)

Yarn Colors and Amounts:
Color A: 400 (500) g
Color B: 500 (600) g

Color Suggestions:
1A: Yellow 125
1B: Brown 110

2A: White 101
2B: Red 124

3A: White 101
3B: Blue 149

4A: Gray 104
4B: Gray 114

Needles: U. S. sizes 1.5 and 2.5 / 2.5 and 3 mm: short and long circulars and sets of 5 dpn

GAUGE

24 sts and 32 rnds in stockinette pattern on larger needles = 4 x 4 in / 10 x 10 cm.
Adjust needle sizes to obtain correct gauge if necessary.

BODY

With Color B and smaller circular, CO 200 (240) sts. Join, being careful not to twist cast-on row. Pm for beginning of rnd. Work around in stockinette for 1¼ (1¼) in / 3 (3) cm for facing.
Make an eyelet rnd for picot foldline: (k2tog, yo) around. Knit 1 rnd.
Change to larger circular and Color A. Knit 2 rnds with A, *at the same time* increasing 2 sts at each side = 204 (244) sts.
Now begin lice pattern: K1 Color A, k1 Color B, alternating colors on every other rnd for about 1 in / 2.5 cm.
Knit 2 rnds with Color A, increasing 2 sts at each side = 208 (248) sts.
Knit 2 rnds with Color B and then 2 rnds with Color A, 4 rnds with Color B and then 2 rnds Color A, increasing 2 sts at each side = 212 (252) sts.
Next, knit 2 rnds Color B, 2 rnds Color A, 2 rnds lice with A/B, and 2 rnds Color A, increasing 2 (3) sts at each side = 216 (258) sts.
Work Panel 1 and then 2 rnds Color A, increasing evenly spaced on last rnd to 218 (266) sts.
Work pattern for body: Panel at side over 10 sts, 15 (19) pattern repeats over 89 (113) sts. The last pattern repeat ends when 1 st remains so the pattern is the same at each side. The panel at side is worked 2 times over 20 sts.
= 15 (19) pattern repeats and panel at side.
Continue with this pattern, and *at the same* time increase at each side as shown on chart, until there are a total of 250 (298) sts.
Continue until body measures approx. 21¾ (24) in / 55 (61) cm, including facing. Knit 1 rnd with Color A and then 39 (49) sts from side (see side sts on chart); place 47 (51) sts on a holder and CO 47 (51) sts.
Knit until 24 sts rem on rnd and increase 1 st; knit to end of rnd. Begin Panel 2. Knit the 47 (51) sts for neck with lice all around, leaving the first 2 sts and last 2 sts in Color A.

The panels should match on each side of the neck. Complete Panel 2, knit 2 rnds with Color A, and then work Panel 3. End with 1 rnd Color A, and then place 39 (49) sts on each side on a holder for shoulders. BO 47 (51) sts at center front. Place 47 (51) sts at center back on a holder.

NECKBAND

Join shoulders. Machine-stitch to reinforce neck, from shoulder down to the neckline, about 1 in / 2.5 cm in on the section with lice. Cut open just outside the stitching line. Fold the edge to the wrong side between the 2 sts in Color A. Sew down as a facing. Pick up and knit sts on the folded edge, making sure there will be 1 row of sts in Color A between the new sts and the pattern on the body. With Color A, knit 1 rnd all around the neckline, decreasing at each of the 4 corners with k2tog. BO. There should be 2 rnds Color A all around the neck (see drawing below).

SLEEVES

Make both alike. With Color B and smaller dpn, CO 48 (58) sts. Divide sts onto dpn and join; pm for beginning of rnd. Work around in k1, p1 ribbing for 1½ in / 4 cm. Change to larger dpn and Color A. On first rnd, increase evenly spaced around to 60 (72) sts.

Knit 1 rnd with Color A and then work in pattern as for main pattern of body. *At the same time*, increase sts centered on underarm on every 4th rnd until there are a total of 130 (140) sts and sleeve is approx. 19 (23¾) in / 48 (60) cm long.

Turn sleeve inside out and work around in stockinette for approx. ¾ in / 2 cm for facing. BO loosely.

ATTACHING SLEEVES

Measure the width of the sleeve top, and then measure the same length down from shoulder seam on body. Pm at base of underarm. Machine-stitch on each side of first st with Color B in striped section, from the pattern on the body, until about 2½ in / 6 cm rem to the marker for depth of armhole. Round off the machine-stitching so it meets in the side sts (center st) of the striped section. Sew a fine zigzag line over the first stitching. Carefully cut steek up center. Attach sleeves with RS facing. Fold facings to WS and sew down.

Weave in all ends neatly on WS.

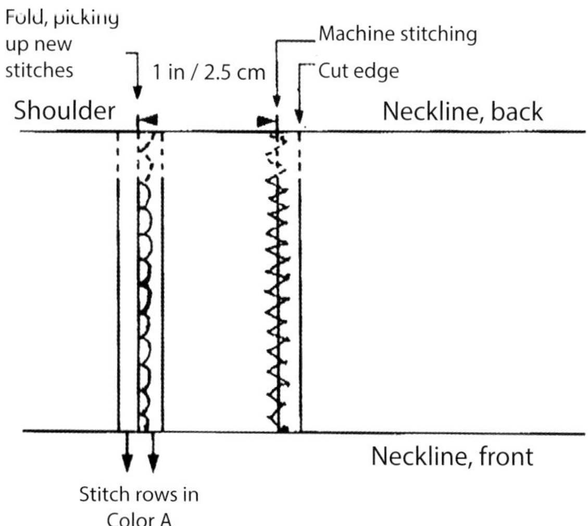

Rather Easy

Easiest is often the best. Or at least that's what I've heard! So in this section we keep it simple: stripes or a single color, and stockinette or only a hint of texture. So easy that, without any special challenges, these patterns can be knitted while you relax and watch the TV series you absolutely must see. Or maybe while you sit on the bus on the way to work. Or when you are out for coffee—or my preference, tea—with a friend.

Lise's Striped Pullover

Bulky yarn + big needles = soon finished! Lise's Striped Pullover is a good project for a beginner—or when you just want a lovely, easy-to-wear garment in no time flat.

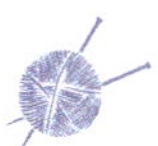

Design: Rauma Garn / Tuva Tokle
Photos: Siren Lauvdal

PROJECT SUMMARY

- A pullover with a puff sleeves
- Worked from the bottom up
- Stockinette pattern—with ribbing at lower edges of body and sleeves, and around the neckline
- Irregular stripe pattern on body and sleeves
- The body is knitted in the round up to the underarms and then divided; the front and back are worked separately above underarms
- EEach sleeve is worked in the round to the underarm and bound off straight across; the sleeves are sewn into the armholes later

SKILL LEVEL

Intermediate

SIZES

XS (S, M, L, XL, XXL)

FINISHED MEASUREMENTS

Chest: approx. 40½ (43¼, 46, 48¾, 51½, 54¾) in / 103 (110, 117, 124, 131, 139) cm
Total Length: approx. 21¼ (22, 22¾, 23¾, 24½, 25¼) in / 54 (56, 58, 60, 62, 64) cm
Sleeve Length: approx. 17¼ (17¼, 17¾, 17¾, 18¼, 18¼) in / 44 (44, 45, 45, 46, 46) cm

MATERIALS

Yarn: CYCA #5 (bulky) Rauma Vams PT3 (100% Norwegian wool, 90 yd/83 m / 50 g)

Yarn Colors and Amounts:
Gray Heather V13: 200 (200, 250, 250, 250, 250) g
Dark Gray-Blue V58: 150 (150, 150, 200, 200, 200) g
Natural V01: 100 (100, 150, 150, 150, 150) g
Light Purple V71: 50 (50, 50, 50, 50, 50) g
Beige V55: 50 (50, 50, 50, 50, 50) g

Needles: U. S. sizes 9 and 10 / 5.5 and 6 mm: circulars and sets of 5 dpn

GAUGE

14 sts in stockinette on larger needles = 4 in / 10 cm in width.
Adjust needle sizes to obtain correct gauge if necessary.

STRIPE PATTERN A (BODY):

3 rnds Light Purple and then Dark Gray-Blue until piece measures 5¼ (5¼, 5¼, 5½, 5½, 5½) in / 13 (13, 13, 14, 14, 14) cm.
3 rnds Beige, 5 rnds Dark Gray-Blue, and then Gray Heather until piece measures 8¼ (8¾, 8¾, 9, 9, 9½) in / 21 (22, 22, 23, 23, 24) cm.
5 rnds Dark Gray-Blue, 7 rnds Gray Heather, 3 rnds Beige, and then Gray Heather until work measures 13¾ (14½, 15, 15¾, 16¼, 16½) in / 16, 35 (37, 38, 40, 41, 42) cm (don't forget the armholes).
3 rows Dark Gray-Blue, 5 rows Natural, 5 rows Dark Gray-Blue, and then Natural to finished length.

STRIPE PATTERN B (SLEEVES):
7 rnds Gray Heather, 3 rnds Beige, 5 rnds Gray Heather, 3 rnds Beige, 10 rnds Gray Heather, 5 rnds Dark Gray-Blue, and then Gray Heather until sleeve measures 14¼ (14¼, 14½, 14½, 15, 15) in / 36 (36, 37, 37, 38, 38) cm.
5 rnds Natural, 3 rnds Gray Heather, and then Natural to finished length.

BODY

With Dark Gray-Blue and smaller circular, CO 144 (152, 164, 172, 184, 192) sts. Join, being careful not to twist cast-on row. Pm for beginning of rnd. Work around in k2, p2 ribbing for 2¾ in / 7 cm (all sizes). Change to larger circular. Knit 1 rnd, increasing 0 (2, 0, 2, 0, 2) sts evenly spaced around = 144 (154, 164, 174, 184, 194) sts. Work around in stockinette and stripe pattern A (see above). *At the same time*, when body measures 13 (13½, 13¾, 14¼, 14½, 15) in / 33 (34, 35, 36, 37, 38) cm, divide for front and back with 72 (77, 82, 87, 92, 97) sts each for front and back. Work each side separately.

FRONT

Continue back and forth in stockinette and Stripe Pattern A until armhole measures 6¼ (6¾, 7, 7½, 8, 8¼) in / 16 (17, 18, 19, 20, 21) cm. Change to smaller needle and Natural. Work in k2, p2 ribbing, and on first row adjust stitch count to 74 (78, 82, 86, 94, 98) sts. When armhole depth is 8¼ (8¾, 9, 9½, 9¾, 10¼) in / 21 (22, 23, 24, 25, 26) cm, BO all sts knitwise on RS.

BACK

Work back as for front.

SLEEVES

Make both alike. With Dark Gray-Blue and smaller dpn, CO 28 sts (all sizes). Divide sts onto dpn and join. Pm for beginning of rnd. Work around in k2, p2 ribbing for 1¼ in / 3 cm (all sizes). Change to larger dpn. Knit 1 rnd, increasing as follows: (K1, yo) around = 56 sts. On next rnd, work all yarnovers as k1tbl. Continue around in stockinette. When sleeve measures 2 in / 5 cm, begin Stripe Pattern B (see above). *At the same time*, increase 2 sts centered on underarm. Increase the same way approx. every 5½ (4, 3¼, 2½, 2½, 1½) in / 14 (10, 8, 6, 6, 4) cm a total of 2 (3, 4, 6, 7, 9) times = 60 (62, 64, 68, 70, 74) sts. Continue in stripe pattern until sleeve measures 17¼ (17¼, 17¾, 17¾, 18¼, 18¼) in / 44 (44, 45, 45, 46, 46) cm. BO loosely.

FINISHING

Seam shoulders, leaving 10¼ (11, 11, 11¾, 11¾, 11¾) in / 26 (28, 28, 30, 30, 30) cm open at center for neck. Attach sleeves.

At-Home Cardigan

Total honesty here: I could move into this cardigan. Long and roomy, with practical pockets. It goes with pants or dresses, for everyday wear or when you want to look nice. What's not to love?

Design: Rauma Garn / Tuva Tokle
Photos: Siren Lauvdal

PROJECT SUMMARY

- Long jacket with pockets, V-neck, shapes armholes, sleeve caps, and shaped shoulders
- Worked from the bottom up
- Stockinette pattern—with ribbing on all edges; the sleeve ribbing is worked in a contrast color and yarn, and the front ribbed bands are worked at the same time as front and back
- The body and sleeves are worked separately to the underarms; then, all the pieces are placed on one needle and the yoke is worked back and forth, while at the same time, the V-neck, armholes and sleeve caps are shaped, and once the sleeve caps are finished, the fronts and back are each worked separately
- The sleeves are increased up the underarms with visible yarnover holes

SKILL LEVEL

Intermediate

SIZES

XS (S, M, L, XL, XXL)

FINISHED MEASUREMENTS

Chest: 45¼ (47¼, 49¼, 51¼, 53¼, 55¼) in / 115 (120, 125, 130, 135, 140) cm

Total Length: 34 (34¾, 35½, 36¼, 37, 37¾) in / 86 (88, 90, 92, 94, 96) cm

Sleeve Length: 17¼ (17¼, 17¼, 17¼, 17¼, 17¼) in / 44 (44, 44, 44, 44, 44) cm

MATERIALS

Yarn:

CYCA #5 (bulky) Rauma Vams PT3 (100% Norwegian wool, 90 yd/83 m / 50 g)

CYCA #1 (fingering) Rauma Concorde (64% rayon/viscose, 36% polyester, 137 yd/125 m / 25 g)

Yarn Colors and Amounts for Beige Jacket:

MC: Vams PT3, Beige V55: 600 (650, 700, 700, 750, 800) g

Vams PT3, Dark Blue V67: leftovers or a 50 g ball

Concorde, Copper 24: 25 (25, 25, 25, 25, 25) g

Concorde, Black/Silver 22: 25 (25, 25, 25, 25, 25) g

Yarn Colors and Amounts for Petroleum Jacket:

MC: Vams PT3, Petroleum V47: 600 (650, 700, 700, 750, 800) g

Concorde, Copper 24: 25 (25, 25, 25, 25, 25) g

Concorde, Gold 20: 25 (25, 25, 25, 25, 25) g

Needles: U. S. sizes 9 and 10 / 5.5 and 6 mm: circulars + U S. 7 and 10 / 4.5 and 6 mm: sets of 5 dpn

GAUGE

14 sts in stockinette on larger needles = 4 in / 10 cm in width.

Adjust needle sizes to obtain correct gauge if necessary.

Knitting Tips: If you don't want to use glitter thread in your jacket, you can substitute Vams PT3 for Concorde.

BODY

With MC and smaller circular, CO 169 (175, 183, 191, 197, 205) sts. Work back and forth in k1, p1 ribbing for 4¾ in / 12 cm (all sizes). Change to larger circular. Continue ribbing over the first and last 8 sts throughout (= front bands; working them with the body means they will be a bit firmer). Work in stockinette over rem sts of body. When body measures 11¾ (12¾, 13½, 13¾, 14¼, 15) in / 30 (32, 34, 35, 36, 38) cm, work as follows: Work 16 (17, 18, 19, 20, 21) sts, place next 19 sts on a holder (for pocket opening) and CO 19 new sts over gap, work until 35 (36, 37, 38, 39, 40) sts rem, place next 19 sts on a holder (for pocket opening) and CO 19 new sts over gap, work as est to end of row. Work all new sts in stockinette. When body measures 26 (26½, 26¾, 27¼, 27½, 28) in / 66 (67, 68, 69, 70, 71) cm, pm at each side with 81 (83, 87, 91, 95, 99) sts for back and 44 (46, 48, 50, 51, 53) sts for each front. On next row (RS), BO 6 sts at each side for armholes. Set body aside while you knit sleeves.

SLEEVES

Make both alike.

Beige Jacket: With smaller dpn, holding one strand each Copper and Black/Silver Concorde together, CO 34 (34, 36, 36, 38, 38) sts. Divide sts onto dpn and join. Work 4 rnds k1, p1 ribbing. Change to Dark Blue Vams. Work 1 rnd ribbing. Change back to one strand each Copper and Black/Silver Concorde. Knit 1 rnd and then work 4 rnds in ribbing.

Petroleum Jacket: With smaller dpn, holding one strand each Copper and Gold Concorde together, CO 34 (34, 36, 36, 38, 38) sts. Divide sts onto dpn and join. Work 4 rnds k1, p1 ribbing. Change to MC. Work 1 rnd ribbing. Change back to one strand each Copper and Gold Concorde. Knit 1 rnd and then work 4 rnds in ribbing.

Both Models: Change to larger dpn and MC. Knit around in stockinette, working the 6th rnd as follows: K14 (14, 15, 15, 16, 16), yo, pm, k6, pm, yo, knit to end of rnd. On next rnd, knit yarnovers as usual to make holes. Continue increasing with a yarnover before first marker and after second marker, on every 5th rnd, a total of 7 (8, 8, 9, 9, 10) times = 48 (50, 52, 54, 56, 58) sts. Continue without further shaping until sleeve is

17¼ in / 44 cm (all sizes) in long. BO 6 sts centered on underarm. Place rem sts on holder.

YOKE

NOTE: Read all the way through this section before you begin knitting.

Place sleeves and body on larger circular, matching underarms = 241 (251, 263, 275, 285, 297) sts total. Pm at each intersection of sleeve and body = 4 markers. Work back and forth in stockinette with the 1st row on WS. *At the same time*, on the first RS row, decrease for both armholes and neck as follows:

Neck Shaping: Decrease inside the 8 ribbing sts for front band at each side on every 3rd row a total of 12 (13, 14, 14, 14, 15) times.

On RS: Work 8 band sts in ribbing, sl 1 knitwise, k1, psso. Knit until 10 sts rem, k2tog, work rem 8 sts in ribbing = 2 sts decreased.

On WS: Work 8 band sts in ribbing, p2tog. Knit until 10 sts rem, p2tog tbl, work rem 8 sts in ribbing = 2 sts decreased.

At the same time, shape armholes as follows:

Work until 2 sts before first marker, sl 1 knitwise, k1, psso, sl m, k2tog. Rep at all markers = 8 sts decreased across. Decrease the same way on every other row a total of 11 (12, 13, 15, 16, 17) times.

Continue decreasing the same way for the sleeves but not on front or back, on every other row a total of 2 (2, 2, 1, 1, 1) times. On next row, BO rem 16 sleeve sts on each side (or place sts on holders). Work each side separately

BACK

CO 1 new st (= edge st which is always knitted on all rows). Work back and forth in stockinette for 1¼ in / 3 cm. Shape shoulders beginning on WS, as follows:

Row 1 (WS): K1 (edge st), p2tog, purl until 3 sts rem, p2tog tbl, k1 (edge st).

Row 2 (RS): K1 (edge st), sl 1 knitwise, k1, psso, knit until 3 sts rem, k2tog, k1 (edge st).

Rep Rows 1-2 until you've decreased 10 times on each shoulder.

On next row, BO rem sts.

FRONT

At armhole, CO 1 new st (= edge st which is always knitted on all rows). Work back and forth in stockinette for 3¼ in / 8 cm from back/front division. BO edge st + the 10 shoulder sts. Place front band sts on a holder. Work the other front the same way.

FINISHING

Join shoulder seams inside the front shaping and inside the edge sts on back. Sew sleeve top (the 16 held/bound-off sts) to shoulder the same way. The shoulder seams will fall slightly back on the sleeve. Place sts of one front band on needle and continue in ribbing as est until band reaches center back neck when slightly stretched. BO. Work the other band the same way. Seam bands and sew down along back neck. Seam underarms.

POCKET EDGINGS

Place held sts on smaller circular. With MC, work across in p1, k1 ribbing for 1¼ in / 3 cm. BO in ribbing. Sew sides of pocket edgings to sweater.

POCKET LININGS

With MC and larger needles, pick up and knit 1 st in each st across = 19 sts. Work back and forth in stockinette for 6¼ in / 16 cm. BO. Sew lining with loose sts on inside of front so it's not visible on RS of sweater.

Men's Striped Pullover

A manly high-necked pullover! The same easy pattern as before, knitted in different colors and with a different stripe sequence. Let yourself play with the colors and stripes—the possibilities are endless.

Design: Rauma Garn / Cecilie Tofthagen
Photos: Rauma Garn

PROJECT SUMMARY

- A pullover with a high neck
- Worked from the bottom up
- Stockinette with ribbed neckband
- The body is knitted in the round up to the underarms and then divided, with stitches bound off for underarms, the front and back are worked separately, back and forth, without further armhole shaping
- Each sleeve is worked in the round to the underarm, and then the sleeve cap is worked back and forth; the sleeves are sewn into the armholes later

SKILL LEVEL

Intermediate

SIZES

XS (S, M, L, XL, XXL)

FINISHED MEASUREMENTS

Chest: 36¾ (38¼, 40½, 43, 45¾, 48½) in / 93 (97, 103, 109, 116, 123) cm
Total Length: 26 (27¼, 28¼, 29¼, 30, 30¾) in / 66 (69, 72, 74, 76, 78) cm
Sleeve Length: 19¼ (19¾, 20, 20½, 21, 21¼) in / 49 (50, 51, 52, 53, 54) cm

MATERIALS

Yarn: CYCA #5 (bulky) Rauma Vams PT3 (100% Norwegian wool, 90 yd/83 m / 50 g)

Yarn Colors and Amounts for Blue/Green Pullover:
Petroleum V47: 100 (150, 150, 150, 200, 200) g
Forest Green V87: 100 (100, 150, 150, 150, 150) g
Khaki Green V89: 100 (100, 100, 100, 150, 150) g
Dark Gray-Blue V58: 100 (100, 100, 100, 150, 150) g
Light Blue V49: 50 (100, 100, 100, 100, 150) g
Light Green V81: 50 (50, 50, 50, 100, 100) g

Yarn Colors and Amounts for Beige/Brown Pullover:
Beige Heather V06: 150 (200, 200, 200, 250, 250) g
Camel V63: 100 (150, 150, 150, 200, 200) g
Beige V55: 100 (100, 100, 100, 150, 150) g
Gray Heather V13: 50 (50, 50, 100, 100, 100) g
Light Gray Heather V03: 50 (50, 50, 50, 100, 100) g
Dark Brown Heather V64: 50 (50, 50, 50, 100, 100) g

Needles: U. S. size 10 / 6 mm: circular and set of 5 dpn

GAUGE

14 sts in stockinette = 4 in / 10 cm in width.
Adjust needle sizes to obtain correct gauge if necessary.

CAST-ON COLOR

Blue/Green pullover: Forest Green
Beige/Brown pullover: Beige

NECKBAND COLOR

Blue/Green pullover: Petroleum
Beige/Brown pullover: Beige Heather

BODY

With cast-on color (see previous page) and circular, CO 130 (136, 144, 152, 162, 172) sts. Join, being careful not to twist cast-on row. Pm for beginning of rnd and at side = 65 (68, 72, 76, 81, 86) sts each for front and back. Work around in stockinette and stripes following chart for Pattern A for chosen size. *At the same time*, when body measures 18¼ (19, 19¾, 20, 20½, 21¼) in / 46 (48, 50, 51, 52, 54) cm, BO 6 sts centered at each side (= 3 sts on each side of each marker) = 59 (62, 66, 70, 75, 80) sts rem on each side. Now work front and back separately.

BACK

Shape armholes at each side: on every other row, decrease 1,1 st = 55 (58, 62, 66, 71 76) sts rem. When armhole depth measures 7 (7½, 8, 8¼, 8¾, 8¾) in / 18 (19, 20, 21, 22, 22) cm, BO the center 15 (16, 16, 16, 17, 18) sts for back neck. Work each side separately. Continue shaping neck: on every other row, BO 2 sts once = 18 (19, 21, 23, 25, 27) sts rem. When armhole depth measures 8 (8¼, 8¾, 9, 9½, 9½) in / 20 (21, 22, 23, 24, 24) cm, BO rem sts.

FRONT

Continue back and forth in stockinette and as for back. When armhole measures 5¼ (5½, 6, 6¼, 6¾, 6¾) in / 13 (14, 15, 16, 17, 17) cm, BO the center 11 (12, 12, 12, 13, 14) sts for front neck. Work each side separately. Continue shaping neck: on every other row, BO 2,2,1 sts = 18 (19, 21, 23, 25, 27) sts rem. BO rem sts when front armhole depth is same as for back.

SLEEVES

Make both alike. With cast-on color and dpn, CO 34 (35 (38, 40, 41, 41) sts. Divide sts onto dpn and join. Pm for beginning of rnd. Work around in stockinette stripes following chart for Pattern A. *At the same time*, every 1½ in / 4 cm, increase 2 sts centered on underarm a total of 11 (12, 12, 12, 13, 13) times = 56 (59, 62, 64, 67, 67) sts. Continue in stripe pattern until sleeve measures 19¼ (19¾, 20, 20½, 21, 21¼) in / 49 (50, 51, 52, 53, 54) cm (Pattern A will not be complete yet, at this point). BO 6 sts centered on underarm. Now work back and forth, decreasing 1 st at each side on every other row 2 times. BO rem sts.

FINISHING

Join shoulders (with three-needle bind-off or mattress st). Attach sleeves.

NECKBAND

With RS facing and neckband color (see previous page), pick up and knit 60 (64, 64, 64, 64, 68) sts around neck. Join and work around in k2, p2 ribbing for 3¼ (3¼, 3¼, 4, 4, 4) in / 8 (8, 8, 10, 10, 10) cm. Increase 1 st in each purl column so each p2 becomes p3. Continue in k2, p3 ribbing until neckband measures 7 (7, 7, 8¾, 8¾, 8¾) in / 18 (18, 18, 22, 22, 22) cm. BO loosely in ribbing.

Weave in all ends neatly on WS.

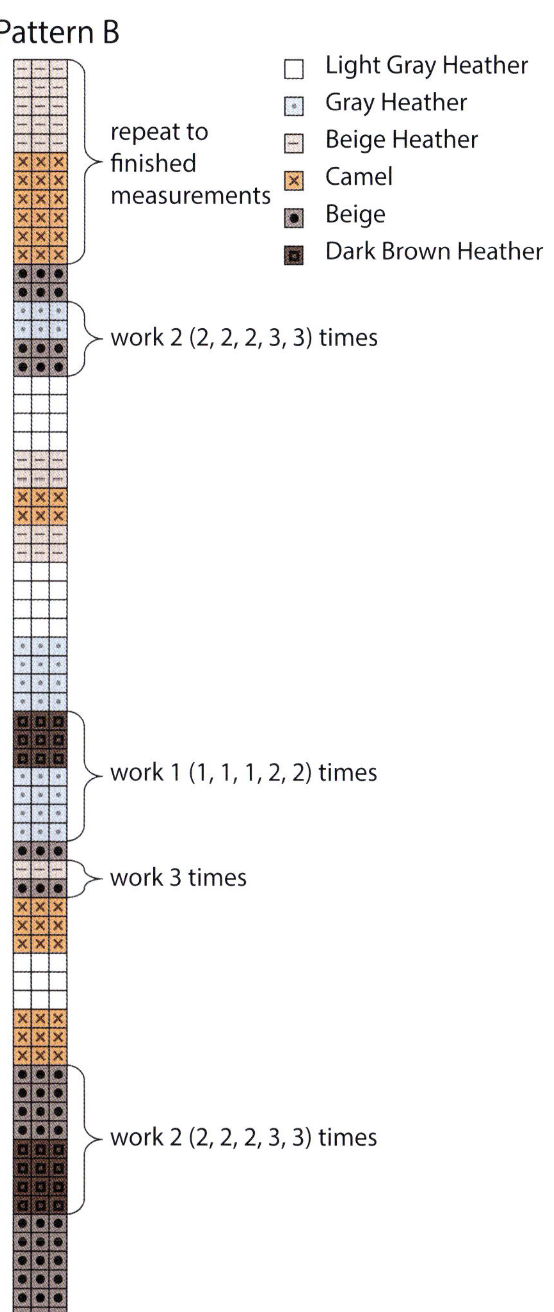

Comfy Pullover and Cozy Pants

Some garments are just so heart-warming! They feel like a soft hug when you need it most. Here's a pair of soothing garments—for those days when you could use a little comfort.

Design: Rauma Garn / Stina Fredriksson
Photos: Pudder Agency / Julie Pike

PROJECT SUMMARY—PULLOVER

- Stockinette, with ribbing at center front
- Shaped shoulders
- Worked from the bottom up
- Ribbing at lower edge of body and sleeves and around neckline
- The body is worked in the round to the underarms; then the front and back are each worked separately, back and forth
- Each sleeve is worked in the round to the underarm, and then the sleeve cap is worked back and forth; the finished sleeves are attached to the armholes later

PROJECT SUMMARY—PANTS

- Pants with ribbing
- Worked from the bottom up
- The legs are worked separately in the round, and then joined on one circular for completion
- Ribbing at lower edges of each leg and around top of pants
- Waist casing for elastic band at top

PULLOVER

SKILL LEVEL

Intermediate

SIZES

XS (S, M, L, XL, XXL)

FINISHED MEASUREMENTS

Chest: 36 (38¼, 41¼, 44, 47¼, 49¾) in / 91 (97, 105, 112, 120, 126) cm

Total Length: 23¼ (24, 24¾, 25½, 26½, 27¼) in / 59 (61, 63, 65, 67, 69) cm

Sleeve Length: 19¼ (19¼, 19¾, 19¾, 20, 20) in / 49 (49, 50, 50, 51, 51) cm

MATERIALS

Yarn: CYCA #2 (sport, baby) Rauma Finull (100% Norwegian wool, 191 yd/175 m / 50 g)

Yarn Colors and Amounts:
Old Rose 4571 or Dark Denim 443: 350 (400, 450, 500, 550, 600) g

Needles: U. S. sizes 1.5 and 2. 5 / 2.5 and 3 mm: circulars and sets of 5 dpn

GAUGE

26 sts in stockinette on larger needles = 4 in / 10 cm in width.
Adjust needle sizes to obtain correct gauge if necessary.

BODY

With smaller circular, CO 236 (252, 272, 292, 312, 328) sts. Join, being careful not to twist cast-on row; pm for beginning of rnd. Work around in k2, p2 ribbing for 2½ in / 6 cm. Change to larger circular. Work next rnd as follows: K30 (32, 35, 38, 41, 43) sts, k2, p2 ribbing over 58 (62, 66, 70, 74, 78) sts (= center front), knit to end of rnd.

Continue as est until body measures 15¾ (16¼, 16½, 17, 17¼, 17¾) in / 40 (41, 42, 43, 44, 45) cm. BO 6 (8, 10, 12, 14, 16) sts centered at each side for underarms = 112 (118, 126, 134, 142, 148) sts rem each for front and back. Work each side separately.

BACK

Work back and forth. Shape armholes at each side: on every other row, decrease 1 st 0 (1, 2, 3, 4, 5) times = 112 (116, 122, 128, 134, 138) sts rem. When armhole depth is 6¾ (7, 7½ 8, 8¼, 8¾) in / 17 (18, 19, 20, 21, 22) cm, place the center 30 (32, 34, 36, 38, 40) sts on a holder for back neck and work each side separately. Now shape neck and shoulders on every other row as follows:

Neck: BO 4 sts once and 2 sts 3 times.

Shaped Shoulder: BO 6 (7, 7, 6, 6, 6) sts 4 (4, 4, 5, 5, 5) times.

BO rem sts. Work the other side to correspond.

FRONT

Work back and forth and shape underarms as for back. When armhole depth is 5¼ in / 13 cm, place the center 30 (32, 34, 36, 38, 40) sts on a holder for front neck and work each side separately. Pm on first and last purl sts of ribbing. Shape neck on RS rows as follows:

Left side: Work in stockinette until 4 sts before marker, k2tog, k2. Work knit over knit and purl over purl to end of row.

Right side: Work in ribbing with knit over knit and purl over purl, k2 after marker, k2tog tbl, continue in stockinette to end of row.

Decrease the same way on every other row a total of 10 times. When armhole depth is 6¾ (7, 7½, 8, 8¼, 8¾) in / 17 (18, 19, 20, 21, 22) cm, shape shoulder on every other row as follows:

BO 6 (7, 7, 6, 6, 6) sts 4 (4, 4, 5, 5, 5) times.

BO rem sts. Work the other side to correspond.

SLEEVES

Make both alike. With smaller dpn, CO 64 (64, 68, 68, 72, 72) sts. Divide sts onto dpn and join. Work around in k2, p2 ribbing for 2½ in / 6 cm. Change to larger dpn. Continue in stockinette, increasing 2 sts centered on underarm. Increase the same way every 1⅜ (1¼, 1, 1, ¾, ¾) in / 3.5 (3, 2.5, 2.5, 2, 2) cm, a total of 12 (14 14, 17, 18, 21) times = 88 (92, 96, 102, 108, 114) sts. When sleeve measures 19¼ (19¼, 19¾, 19¾, 20, 20) in / 49 (49, 50, 50, 51, 51) cm, BO 6 (8, 10, 12, 14, 16) sts centered on underarm = 82 (84, 86, 90, 94, 98) sts rem. Now work back and forth, shaping sleeve cap as follows: BO 3 sts at beginning of row and k2tog at end of row a total of 4 times. BO 2 sts at beginning of row and k2tog at end of row a total of 8 (10, 12, 14, 16, 18) times. BO 4 sts at beginning of row and k2tog at end of row a total of 2 times = 32 (28, 24, 22, 20, 18) sts rem. BO rem sts.

FINISHING

Seam shoulders. Attach sleeves.

NECKBAND

Place held sts onto smaller circular, and additionally pick up and knit about 5-6 sts per ¾ in / 2 cm along straight sides of neck. The total stitch count should be a multiple of 4 sts. Join and work around in k2, p2 ribbing (and make sure it aligns with previous ribbing) for 1¼ in / 3 cm, and then work in stockinette for ⅜ in / 1 cm. BO.

Weave in all ends neatly on WS.

PANTS

SKILL LEVEL

Intermediate

SIZES

XS (S, M, L, XL, XXL)

FINISHED MEASUREMENTS

Hip: 34 (37, 40¼, 43¼, 47¼, 51¼) in / 86 (94, 102, 110, 120, 130) cm.

Total Length: at front, 40½ (41, 41¼, 41¾, 42¼, 42½) in / 103 (104, 105, 106, 107, 108) cm

Inner Leg Length: 30¼ (30¼, 30¾, 30¾, 31, 31) in / 77 (77, 78, 78, 79, 79) cm

MATERIALS

Yarn: CYCA #2 (sport, baby) Rauma Finull (100% Norwegian wool, 191 yd/175 m / 50 g)

Yarn Colors and Amounts:

Old Rose 4571 or Dark Denim 443: 350 (400, 450, 500, 550, 600) g

Needles: U. S. sizes 1.5 and 2. 5 / 2.5 and 3 mm: circulars and sets of 5 dpn

Notions: 2½ in / 6 cm wide waistband elastic, to fit around waist + seam allowance

GAUGE

26 sts in stockinette on larger needles = 4 in / 10 cm in width.

Adjust needle sizes to obtain correct gauge if necessary.

LEGS

With smaller dpn, CO 56 (56, 60, 60, 64, 64) sts. Divide sts onto dpn and join. Move sts to circular when possible. Work around in k2, p2 ribbing for 2½ in / 6 cm. Change to larger dpn. Work 1st rnd as follows: K21, *at the same time* increasing 7 (8, 7, 8, 7, 8) sts evenly spaced across = 28 (29, 28, 29, 28, 29) sts; work 14 (14 18, 18, 22, 22) sts in k2, p2 ribbing, and then k21, *at the same time* increasing 7 (8, 7, 8, 7, 8) sts evenly spaced across = 28 (29, 28, 29, 28, 29) sts. There should now be a total of 70 (72, 74, 76, 78, 80) sts. Work knit over knit and purl over purl for remainder of leg. *At the same time*, increase 2 sts centered on inside of leg approx. every ¾ (⅝, ⅝, ⅝, ⅝, ⅝) in / 2 (1.5, 1.5, 1.5, 1, 1) cm a total of 32 (36, 41, 46, 52, 58) times = 134 (144, 156, 168, 182, 196) sts. When leg measures 30¼ (30¼, 30¾, 30¾, 31, 31) in / 77 (77, 78, 78, 79, 79) cm, BO 12 (12, 13, 13, 14, 15) sts centered on inside of leg = 122 (132, 143, 155, 168, 181) sts rem. Place sts on holder and make second leg the same way.

JOINING LEGS

Place both legs on larger circular with bound-off sts facing each other = 244 (264, 286, 310, 336, 362) sts. Pm at center front and back. Decrease 1 st on each side of each marker on every other rnd 5 (5, 5, 6, 6, 6) times = 224 (244, 266, 286, 312, 338) sts rem. Continue around in stockinette and ribbing as est until pants measure 8 (8¼, 8¼, 8¾, 8¾, 9) in / 20 (21, 21, 22, 22, 23) cm from join. Pm at center back and raise back as follows: Work 9 sts past marker; turn and work 18 sts back. Turn and work 18 sts past marker; turn and work 36 sts back. Continue back and forth the same way with 9 more sts for each turn, a total of 5 times on each side. Work 1 rnd over all sts and then decrease 60 (60, 62, 62, 60, 54) sts evenly spaced across stockinette at front and back = 164 (184, 204, 224, 252, 284) sts rem.

Change to smaller circular. Work around in k2, p2 ribbing for 2½ in / 6 cm (make sure ribbing aligns with ribbing at sides of pants). Purl 1 rnd (= foldline) and then work 2½ in / 6 cm in stockinette for facing. BO.

FINISHING

Fold waist facing to wrong side and sew down, leaving an opening for elastic. Thread elastic through casing and seam short ends of elastic. Finish sewing down casing. Seam crotch. Weave in all ends neatly on WS.

Florina Dress

I dig this dress. It's so simple and stylish. And it couldn't be any better, since I'm wild about green just now! But if you don't want to "go green" with this pattern, there are 133 other options on the color chart—you can probably guess where I'm going with this.

Design: Rauma Garn / Britt Kathrine Aasen
Photos: Siren Lauvdal

PROJECT SUMMARY

- Stockinette dress, with split neck at back, shaped shoulders, fitted shaping, split sleeve edges
- Brioche edgings on sleeves and at top of yoke, stockinette facings on lower edge of skirt, ribbing around neck
- Worked from the bottom up
- Body/skirt are worked in the round to the underarms, and then front and back are each worked separately, back and forth, with rounded armholes
- Each sleeve is worked in the round to the underarm, and then the sleeve cap is worked back and forth; the finished sleeves are attached to the armholes later

SKILL LEVEL

Intermediate/Experienced

SIZES

XS (S, M, L, XL, XXL)

FINISHED MEASUREMENTS

Chest: 29½ (33½, 37, 40½, 44, 48) in / 75 (85, 94, 103, 112, 122) cm
Total Length: 31 (33½, 34¾, 36, 37½, 39) in / 79 (85, 88, 91, 95, 99) cm
Sleeve Length: 15 (15½, 15¾, 16¼, 16½, 17) in / 38 (39, 40, 41, 42, 43) cm

MATERIALS

Yarn: CYCA #2 (sport, baby) Rauma Finull (100% Norwegian wool, 191 yd/175 m / 50 g)

Yarn Colors and Amounts:
Green Heather 4130: 450 (500, 550, 550, 600, 650) g

Needles: U. S. sizes 1.5 and 2. 5 / 2.5 and 3 mm: circulars and sets of 5 dpn

Notions: 1 button

GAUGE

26 sts in stockinette on larger needles = 4 in / 10 cm in width.
Adjust needle sizes to obtain correct gauge if necessary.

BRIOCHE WORKED BACK AND FORTH

Row 1: K1, p1.
Row 2: K1, yo, and *at the same time* slip next st, inserting needle into back of st.
Row 3: K 1 st tog with yarnover of previous row, yo, and *at the same time* slip next st, inserting needle into back of st.
Rep Row 3, with purl over purl and knit over knit.

BODY/SKIRT

With larger circular, CO 236 (260, 284, 308, 332, 356) sts. Join, being careful not to twist cast-on row. Pm for beginning of rnd and at side = 118 (130, 142, 154, 166, 178) sts each for front and back. Work around in stock-

inette for 1¼ in / 3 cm. Purl 1 rnd (= foldline—take all subsequent measurements from foldline). Continue around in stockinette until body measures 3¼ (4, 4¾, 5½, 6¼, 7) in / 8 (10, 12, 14, 16, 18) cm. Decrease 1 st at each side of each marker = 4 sts decreased around. Decrease the same way every 1¼ in / 3 cm a total of 14 times = 180 (204, 228, 252, 276, 300) sts rem. When piece measures 20½ (21¼, 22, 22¾, 23¾, 24½) in / 52 (54, 56, 58, 60, 62) cm, increase 1 st at each side of each marker every ¾ in / 2 cm a total of 4 times = 196 (220, 244, 268, 292, 316) sts. When piece measures 24 (25¼, 26½, 28, 28¾, 30) in / 61 (64, 67, 71, 73, 76) cm, BO 10 sts centered on each side for underarms = 88 (100, 112, 124, 136, 148) sts rem each for front and back. Work each side separately.

BACK

Work back and forth. On every other row, at armhole edge, BO 3 sts once, 2 sts once, 1 st once. Pm at center back. When armhole depth is 2¾ (3¼, 3½, 4, 4¼, 4¾) in / 7 (8, 9, 10, 11, 12) cm, BO 1 st at each side of center back marker for back split; work each side separately. Continue in brioche (see page 54). When armhole depth is 7 (7½, 8, 8¼, 8¾, 9) in / 18 (19, 20, 21, 22, 23) cm, begin shoulder shaping, from shoulder to neck, as follows: BO 4 sts 4 (5, 7, 8, 9, 10) times = 16 (20, 28, 32, 36, 40) sts bound off on each shoulder. Place rem 21 (23, 21, 23, 25, 27) sts on a holder for neck.

FRONT

Shape armhole as for back. When armhole depth is 2¾ (3¼, 3½, 4, 4¼, 4¾) in / 7 (8, 9, 10, 11, 12) cm, begin working in brioche. When armhole measures 4 (4¼, 4¾, 5¼, 5½, 6) in / 10 (11, 12, 13, 14, 15) cm, place the center 20 (24, 20, 24, 28, 32) sts on a holder for neck and work each side separately. At neck edge, on every other row, BO 3 sts once, 2 sts 3 times, 1 st 3 times. When armhole depth is 7 (7½, 8, 8¼, 8¾, 9) in / 18 (19, 20, 21, 22, 23) cm, begin shoulder shaping, from shoulder to neck, as follows: BO 4 sts 4 (5, 7, 8, 9, 10) times. All shoulder sts have now been bound off.

SLEEVES

Make both alike. With smaller short circular, CO 80 (82, 84, 86, 88, 90) sts. Work back and forth in brioche for 6¼ (6¾, 7, 7½, 8, 8¼) in / 16 (17, 18, 19, 20, 21) cm. On next row, k2tog across = 40 (41, 42, 43, 44, 45) sts rem. Change to larger dpn. Join and work around in stockinette. *At the same time*, increase 2 sts centered on underarm every ⅜ (⅜, ⅜, ¼, ¼, ¼) in / 1 (1, 1, .75, .75, .75) cm 21 (22, 23, 25, 26, 27) times = 82 (85, 88, 93, 96, 99) sts. When sleeve is 15 (15½, 15¾, 16¼, 16½, 17) in / 38 (39, 40, 41, 42, 43) cm long, BO 10 sts centered on underarm. Now work back and forth, and *at the same time* shape sleeve cap. On every other row at each side, BO 2 sts 3 times, 1 st 11 times, 2 sts 4 times. BO rem sts.

NECKBAND

With smaller circular, beginning on back, pick up and knit 13 sts per 2 in / 5 cm (the total should be an odd number of sts) around neck. Work back and forth in k1, p1 ribbing for about 3¼ in / 8 cm. BO in ribbing.

FINISHING

Join shoulders. Attach sleeves.
Fold facing on skirt to WS and sew down.
Fold neckband double and sew down. Make a button loop at top of back split, just below neckband. Sew button on opposite side.
Weave in all ends neatly on WS.

GEMS FROM THE ARCHIVE

HUSFLIDEN'S

KNITTING PATTERN No. 860
RAUMA VAMSEGARN
Sizes 36/38—40/42

No. 860 Hooded Cape Poncho

Check it out: this is your poncho! We're taking a look back to the unbeatable 1970s. All very '70s styling, with a high polo neck and flipping bangs, and possibly even foot-shaped shoes.

PROJECT SUMMARY

- Poncho with "pocket" slits at front, button bands, rounded shaping and hood
- Garter stitch edgings at lower edge, pocket openings, and along the button bands / hood
- Worked from the bottom up
- Worked in the round and then back and forth at the pocket openings, button bands, and hood
- The same stripe pattern but different color choices

Hooded Cape Poncho Knitted with Rauma Vamse Yarn

SKILL LEVEL

Intermediate/Experienced

SIZES

36/38 (40/42)

MATERIALS

Yarn: CYCA #5 (bulky) Rauma Vams PT3 (100% Norwegian wool, 3-ply, 90 yd/83 m / 50 g)

Yarn Colors and Amounts for Blue Poncho:
Color A: Blue V59: 500 (650) g
Color B: Purple V96: 100 (100) g
Color C: White V01: 100 (150) g
Color D: Purple V80: 100 (150) g

Yarn Colors and Amounts for Brown Poncho:
Color A: Brown V64: 500 (650) g
Color B: White V01: 100 (100) g
Color C: Brown V11: 100 (150) g
Color D: Beige V06: 100 (150) g

Needles: U.S. size 8 / 5 mm: short and long circulars

Crochet Hook: U. S. size J-8 / 5 mm

Notions: 3 buttons

GAUGE

16 sts in stockinette = 4 in / 10 cm.
Adjust needle size to obtain correct gauge if necessary.

CAPE PONCHO

With Color A, CO 270 (286) sts. Join, being careful not to twist-cast-on row; pm for beginning of rnd. Work around in garter st (= alternate knit and purl rnds) for 10 rnds. Begin stripe pattern (see following page). After every 3½ in / 8 cm, decrease 12 sts evenly spaced around. Decrease the same way until 196 (212) sts rem. When piece measures approx. 13½ (15) in / 34 (38) cm, work back and forth for pockets. Place 60 sts at center front on a holder. Work rem sts back and forth for 6 (6¼) in / 15 (16) cm. Now work the same way over the 60 sts on holder. Don't forget the decreases. Place all the sts on the circular and work around until piece measures approx. 21¾ (23¼) in / 55 (59) cm.

Next, begin working back and forth for front opening. CO 8 extra sts on left side for pocket edge. Work these sts in garter st, back and forth. The 8 outermost sts on right side are worked the same way. Make 3 buttonholes on the right pocket edge, spaced 2 in / 5 cm apart. When piece measures approx. 24¾ (26½) in / 63 (67) cm, begin rounded shaping.

Throughout, the 8 edge sts at each side are not included in the stitch counts listed on the decrease sequence on next page.

Rounded Shaping: Decrease evenly spaced around to 180 (200) sts.
Knit 7 rnds and decrease every 10th st to 162 (180) sts.
Knit 7 rnds and decrease every 9th st to 144 (160) sts.
Knit 7 rnds and decrease every 8th st to 126 (140) sts.
Knit 7 rnds and decrease every 7th st to 108 (120) sts.
Knit 5 rnds and decrease every 5th st to 87 (96) sts.
Knit 3 rnds and decrease evenly spaced around to 72 (80) sts.

Now work hood. The pocket edges continue as an edging around hood.

Every 2½ in / 6 cm, turn work at edge on each side. These short rows makes a firmer edge. Work as est until hood measures approx. 13¾ (14½) in / 35 (37) cm. Divide sts into 2 sets and work 3-needle bind-off from center.

FINISHING

Pick up and knit sts along outermost edge of pocket opening. Work back and forth in garter st (= knit all rows) for 1½ in / 4 cm. Stitch down the overlap of the front placket. Work an edging of single crochet along inner edge of each pocket opening. Sew buttons at neck opening.

STRIPE PATTERN FOR CAPE PONCHO

3 rnds	knit	Color A	
1 rnd	purl	Color B	
1 rnd	knit	Color C	
1 rnd	purl	Color C	
1 rnd	knit	Color D	
1 rnd	purl	Color D	
3 rnds	knit	Color A	
1 rnd	purl	Color B	
1 rnd	knit	Color A	
1 rnd	purl	Color A	
1 rnd	knit	Color A	
1 rnd	purl	Color C	
1 rnd	knit	Color C	
1 rnd	purl	Color C	
3 rnds	knit	Color A	2 times
1 rnd	purl	Color D	
1 rnd	knit	Color D	
1 rnd	purl	Color D	
1 rnd	knit	Color D	
1 rnd	purl	Color C	
1 rnd	knit	Color A	
1 rnd	purl	Color A	
1 rnd	knit	Color A	
1 rnd	purl	Color B	
1 rnd	knit	Color B	
1 rnd	purl	Color B	
3 rnds	knit	Color A	
1 rnd	purl	Color C	
1 rnd	knit	Color D	
1 rnd	purl	Color A	
1 rnd	knit	Color A	
1 rnd	purl	Color A	
1 rnd	knit	Color A	
1 rnd	purl	Color B	
1 rnd	knit	Color B	
1 rnd	purl	Color B	
1 rnd	knit	Color C	
1 rnd	purl	Color C	
3 rnds	knit	Color A	
1 rnd	purl	Color D	
1 rnd	knit	Color D	
1 rnd	purl	Color D	
1 rnd	knit	Color D	
1 rnd	purl	Color C	
8 rnds	knit	Color A	
1 rnd	purl	Color C	
1 rnd	knit	Color C	
1 rnd	purl	Color C	
1 rnd	knit	Color D	
1 rnd	purl	Color A	
4 rnds	knit	Color A	
1 rnd	purl	Color B	
24 rnds	knit	Color A	
1 rnd	purl	Color B	
1 rnd	purl	Color C	
1 rnd	purl	Color B	

Knit rest of piece with Color A

This stripe sequence is set up for knitting on a circular needle. You'll have to adjust when you are working back and forth.

Fitted, Stylized, and a Bit Delicate

Go ahead, you're allowed to be distinctive! Combine colors that are surprising or even ones that clash a little. Test out patterns that are different, peculiar, or whimsical.

Anyway, who was it who decided that pink and rust don't go together, that the pattern on a saucepan can't be used on a sweater—or that a striped dress *must* have stripes?

Wide Brioche Pullover

Brioche—a lot of people who don't knit think this word only refers to a French yeast bread, and their mouths start watering at the thought of it. But if you're a knitting enthusiast, perhaps your circular needles begin to twitch; we love two-color brioche knitting.

Design: Marie Cecilie Dahl
Photos: Hilde Kvivik Kavli

PROJECT SUMMARY

- Pullover with wide sleeves and raglan shaping
- Worked from the bottom up
- Brioche knitting, with ribbing around the neckline and lower edges of body and sleeves
- Body and sleeves worked separately to the underarms; then all the pieces are arranged on a circular so the yoke can be worked in the round

SKILL LEVEL

Experienced

SIZES

S (M, L, XL)

FINISHED MEASUREMENTS

Chest: 52 (55¼, 58¼, 61½) in / 132 (140, 148, 156) cm
Total Length: 19 (19¾, 20½, 21¼) in / 48 (50, 52, 54) cm
Sleeve Length: 13 (13½, 13¾, 14¼) in / 33 (34, 35, 36) cm

MATERIALS

Yarn: CYCA #5 (bulky) Rauma Vams PT3 (100% Norwegian wool, 3-ply, 90 yd/83 m / 50 g)

Yarn Colors and Amounts:
Terracotta V42: 350 (450, 500, 550) g
Pink V60: 200 (250, 300, 350) g

Needles: U.S. sizes 9 and 10½ / 5.5 and 6.5 mm: short and long circulars; sets of 5 dpn

GAUGE

10 sts in brioche on larger needles = 4 in / 10 cm.
Adjust needle sizes to obtain correct gauge if necessary.

BODY

With Terracotta and smaller circular, CO 158 (168, 178, 188) sts. Join, being careful not to twist cast-on row; pm for beginning of rnd. Work around in k1, p1 ribbing for 1¼ in / 3 cm. Change to larger circular. Knit 1 rnd, *at the same time* decreasing 26 (28, 30, 32) sts evenly spaced around = 132 (140, 148, 156) sts rem. Now work in brioche as follows:
Rnd 1 (Pink): (K1 in st below, p1) around.
Rnd 2 (Terracotta): (K1, p1 in st below) around.
Rep Rnds 1-2 until body measures 11¾ (12¾, 13½, 14¼) in / 30 (32, 34, 36) cm. Next, BO 8 sts centered on each side for underarms. Set body aside while you knit sleeves.

SLEEVES

Make both alike. Work in the round. With Terracotta and smaller dpn, CO 44 (46, 48, 50) sts. Divide sts onto dpn and join. Work around in k1, p1 ribbing for 1¼ in / 3 cm. Change to larger dpn. Knit 1 rnd, *at the same*

time increasing 10 (10,10, 10) sts evenly spaced around = 54 (56, 58, 60) sts. Work in brioche as for body. When sleeve measures 13 (13½, 13¾, 14¼) in / 33 (34, 35, 36) cm, BO 8 sts centered on underarm.

YOKE

Arrange body and sleeves on long, larger circular, matching underarms = 208 (220, 232, 244) sts total. Pm at each intersection of sleeve and body = 4 markers. Continue in brioche as est but only with Terracotta.

On the 3rd rnd, begin raglan decreasing as follows: Work until 3 sts before first marker, p2tog, k1, p2tog. Work until 2 sts before next marker, p2tog, k1, p2tog. Decrease the same way at the next two markers = 8 sts decreased around. Decrease the same way on every other rnd a total of 17 (18, 20, 21) times = 72 (76, 72, 76) sts rem. Knit 1 rnd and then decrease 0 (4, 0, 2) sts evenly spaced around = 72 (72, 72, 74) sts rem.

NECKBAND

With Terracotta and smaller circular, work around in k1, p1 ribbing for 2 in / 5 cm. BO in ribbing.

FINISHING

Seam underarms. Weave in all ends neatly on WS.

Round Yoke Pullover with Endless Pattern

Now I can reconnect with the 1960s and '70s! You know—simple, stylized, retro patterns that live forever. Patterns you might find on an enameled bowl, or a large and magnificent teapot, or a kettle in bright, psychedelic colors. Or maybe even on a knitted pullover.

Design: Rauma Garn / Stina Fredriksson
Photos: Pudder Agency / Julie Pike

PROJECT SUMMARY

- Pullover with a round yoke
- Stockinette with ribbing on lower edges of body and sleeves, and around neck
- Worked from the bottom up
- Body and sleeves worked separately to the underarms; then all the pieces are arranged on a circular so the yoke can be worked in the round

SKILL LEVEL

Intermediate/Experienced

SIZES

XS (S, M, L, XL, XXL)

FINISHED MEASUREMENTS

Chest: 34¾ (37, 40¼, 43, 46, 48½) in / 88 (94, 102, 109, 117, 123) cm
Total Length: 22½ (23¼, 24, 24¾, 25½, 26½) in / 57 (59, 61, 63, 65, 67) cm
Sleeve Length: 18¼ (18¼, 18½, 18½, 19, 19) in / 46 (46, 47, 47, 48, 48) cm

MATERIALS

Yarn: CYCA #2 (sport, baby) Rauma Finull (100% Norwegian wool, 191 yd/175 m / 50 g)

Yarn Colors and Amounts:
Natural 401 or Gray-Beige 452: 300 (300, 350, 350, 400, 500) g
Mustard Yellow 4805 or Burgundy 428: 100 (100, 100, 100, 100, 100) g

Needles: U. S. sizes 1.5 and 2. 5 / 2.5 and 3 mm: circulars and sets of 5 dpn

GAUGE

26 sts in stockinette on larger needles = 4 in / 10 cm in width.
Adjust needle sizes to obtain correct gauge if necessary.

BODY

With Natural or Gray-Beige and smaller circular, CO 228 (244, 264, 284, 304, 320) sts. Join, being careful not to twist cast-on row; pm for beginning of rnd. Work around in k2, p2 ribbing for 2½ in / 6 cm. Change to larger circular. Knit around in stockinette until body measures 14½ (15, 15½, 15¾, 16¼, 16¼) in / 37 (38, 39, 40, 41, 41) cm.
BO 8 (8, 10, 10, 12, 12) sts centered at each side for underarms = 106 (114, 122, 132, 140, 148) sts rem

Pattern A

Do not work for sizes XS, S, and M
= 147 (154, 161, 168, 175, 182) sts
= 189 (198, 207, 216, 225, 234) sts
= 231 (242, 253, 264, 275, 286) sts
= 273 (286, 299, 312, 325, 338) sts
Natural or Gray-Beige
Mustard Yellow or Burgundy
k2tog
k2tog tbl
repeat
center back begin here XS / M / XL
center back begin here S / L / XXL

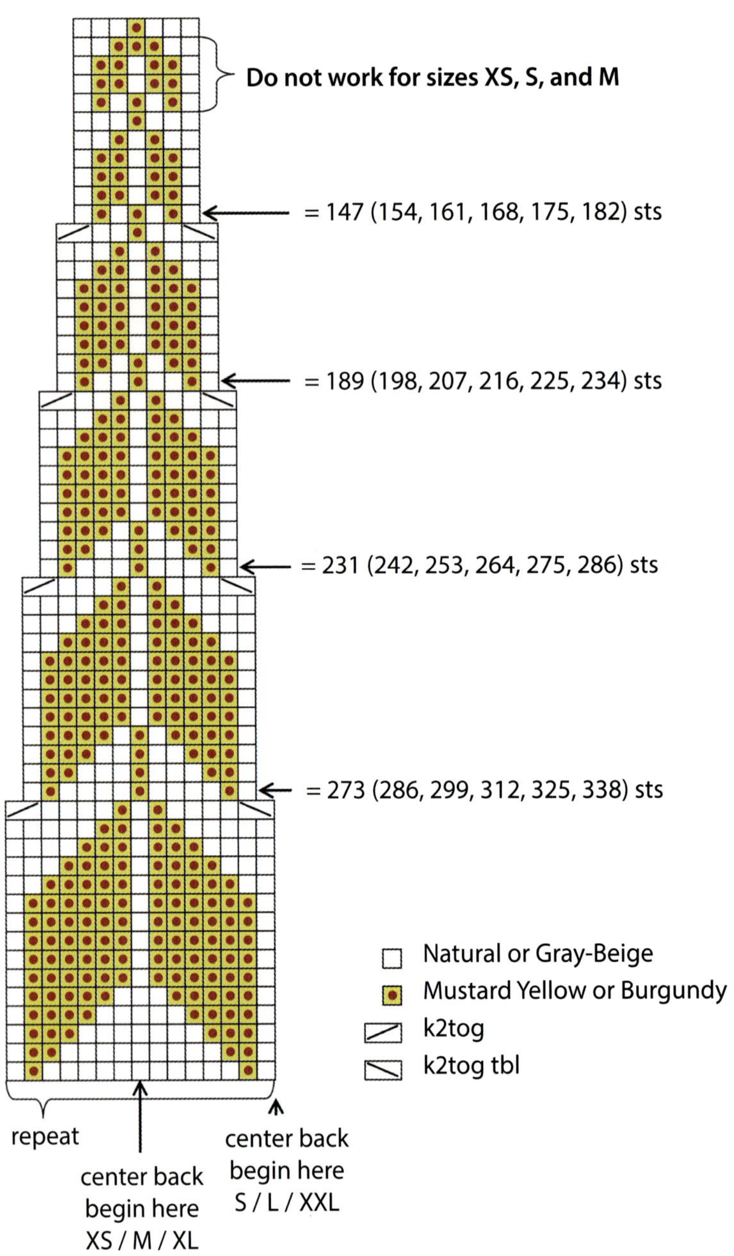

each for front and back. Set body aside while you knit sleeves.

SLEEVES

Make both alike. With Natural or Gray-Beige and smaller dpn, CO 64 (64, 68, 68, 72, 72) sts. Divide sts onto dpn and join. Work around in k2, p2 ribbing for 2½ in / 6 cm. Change to larger dpn and work around in stockinette. At the same time, increase 2 sts centered on underarm. Increase the same way every 1⅜ (1¼, 1¼, 1, 1, ¾) in / 3.5 (3, 3, 2.5, 2.5, 2) cm for a total of 10 (12, 13, 15, 16, 18) increase rnds = 84 (88, 94, 98, 104, 108) sts. When sleeve is 18¼ (18¼, 18½, 18½, 19, 19) in / 46 (46, 47, 47, 48, 48) cm long, BO 8 (8, 10, 10, 12, 12) sts centered on underarm = 76 (80, 84, 88, 92, 96) sts rem.

YOKE

Arrange body and sleeves on long, larger circular, matching underarms = 364 (388, 412, 440, 464, 488) sts total. Pm at each intersection of sleeve and body = 4 markers. Continue in stockinette with Natural or Gray-Beige. On the 2nd rnd, begin raglan decreasing at each marker as follows: Work until 3 sts before marker, k2tog tbl, k2, k2tog = 8 sts decreased around. Decrease the same way on every other rnd a total of 3 (3, 4, 4, 5, 5) times = 340 (364, 380, 408, 424, 448) sts rem. Knit 1 rnd, *at the same time* decreasing 25 (34, 35, 48, 49, 58) sts evenly spaced around = 315 (330, 345, 360, 375, 390) sts rem. Work following chart for Pattern A. After completing charted rows, knit 1 rnd, *at the same time* decreasing 11 (14, 17, 20, 23, 26) sts evenly spaced around = 136 (140, 144, 148, 152, 156) sts rem. Change to smaller circular and continue with Natural or Gray-Beige. Work around in k2, p2 ribbing for 2 in / 5 cm. BO in ribbing.

FINISHING

Seam underarms.
Weave in all ends neatly on WS.

Five-Spot Pullover

We're talking lots of motifs here—meaning panels in abundance! And while a five-spot pattern like this is a common tattoo for the arm or hand, we've chosen here to keep things a little less permanent and knit them all over the sweater instead. Smart!

Design: Rauma Garn
Photos: Henriette Berg-Thomassen

PROJECT SUMMARY

- Pullover with a round neck or V-neck
- Worked from the bottom up
- Stockinette with ribbing on lower edges of body and sleeves, and around neck
- The body is knitted in the round; stitches are bound off for the underarms, and then the front and back are worked separately, back and forth
- The sleeves are worked in the round up to the underarms, and then a short sleeve cap is worked back and forth; the finished sleeves are sewn into the armholes

SKILL LEVEL

Experienced

SIZES

XS (S, M, L, XL, XXL)

FINISHED MEASUREMENTS

Chest: 34¾ (37¾, 41¼, 45, 48½, 51½) in / 88 (96, 105, 114, 123, 131) cm
Total Length: 25½ (26¾, 28¼, 30, 31½, 32¼) in / 65 (68, 72, 76, 80, 82) cm
Sleeve Length: 19¼ (19¾, 20, 20, 20½, 20½) in / 49 (50, 51, 51, 52, 52) cm

MATERIALS

Yarn: CYCA #5 (bulky) Rauma Vams PT3 (100% Norwegian wool, 3-ply, 90 yd/83 m / 50 g)

Yarn Colors and Amounts—Brown Pullover:
MC: Dark Brown Heather V64: 200 (200, 250, 250, 250, 300) g
Light Gray Heather V03: 150 (150, 150, 150, 150, 200) g
Beige V55: 150 (150, 150, 150, 150, 200) g
Charcoal Gray Heather V14: 100 (100, 100, 100 100, 150) g
Gray Heather V13: 100 (100, 100, 100 100, 100) g
Beige Heather V06: 50 (50, 100, 100, 100, 100) g

Yarn Colors and Amounts—Blue Pullover:
MC: Dark Gray-Blue V58: 200 (200, 250, 250, 250, 300) g
Khaki Green V89: 150 (150, 150, 150, 150, 200) g
Denim V51: 150 (150, 150, 150, 150, 200) g
Dark Petroleum V53: 100 (100, 100, 100 100, 150) g
Forest Green V87: 100 (100, 100, 100 100, 100) g
Light Denim V50: 50 (50, 100, 100, 100, 100) g

Needles: U. S. sizes 9 and 10½-11 / 5.5 and 7 mm: circulars and sets of 5 dpn

GAUGE

16 sts in stockinette pattern on larger needles = 4 in / 10 cm in width.
NOTE: If you knit more tightly in two-color stranded knitting than in a single color, go up a needle size for the stranded colorwork.
Adjust needle sizes to obtain correct gauge if necessary.

BODY

With MC and smaller circular, CO 140 (154, 168, 182, 196, 210) sts. Join, being careful not to twist cast-on row; pm for beginning of rnd and at side = 70 (77, 84,

91, 98, 105) sts each for front and back. Work around in k1, p1 ribbing for 2½ in / 6 cm. Change to larger circular. Knit around in Pattern A for your chosen size, as follows: begin at side, at arrow for your size, on both front and back (that is, at both markers). When body measures 17¼ (18¼, 19¼, 20½, 21¾, 22½) in / 44 (46, 49, 52, 55, 57) cm, work the next rnd as: BO 3 (3, 4, 4, 5, 5) sts for underarm, k65 (71, 77, 83, 89, 95) (= front), BO 5 (6, 7, 8, 9, 10) for underarm, k65 (71, 77, 83, 89, 95) (= back), BO rem 2 (3, 3, 4, 4, 5) sts. Now work front and back separately.

BACK

Work back and forth. Shape armholes by decreasing at each side on every other row: BO 2 sts once, 1 st 0 (1,1, 2, 2, 3) times = 61 (65, 71, 75, 81, 85) sts rem. When armhole depth is 7½ (8, 8¼, 8¾, 9, 9) in / 19 (20, 21, 22, 23, 23) cm, BO the center 21 (21, 21, 23, 23, 23) sts for back neck. Work each side separately. Work one row without decreasing; on next row, BO another 2 sts once = 18 (20, 23, 24, 27, 29) sts rem for shoulder. When armhole measures 8¼ (8¾, 9, 9½, 9¾, 9¾) in / 21 (22, 23, 24, 25, 25) cm, BO rem sts.

FRONT WITH ROUND NECK

Work back and forth and shape armhole as for back. When armhole measures 5¼ (5½, 6, 6¼, 6¾, 6¾) in / 13 (14, 15, 16, 17, 17) cm, BO the center 17 (17, 17, 19, 19, 19) sts for front neck. Work each side separately. On every other row, at neck edge, BO 2 sts once, 1 st 2 times = 18 (20, 23, 24, 27, 29) sts rem for shoulder. When front is same length as back, BO rem sts.

FRONT WITH V-NECK

BO the center st for base of V-neck and work each side separately.

Work back and forth and shape armhole as for back. *At the same time*, shape V-neck at neck edge: on every other row, decrease 1 st 10 times and then on every 4th row 2 (2, 2, 3, 3, 3) times = 18 (20, 23, 24, 27, 29) sts rem for shoulder. When front is same length as back, BO rem sts. Work opposite side to correspond.

SLEEVES

Make both alike. With MC and smaller dpn, CO 30 (34, 34, 34, 36, 36) sts. Divide sts onto dpn and join. Work around in k1, p1 ribbing for 1½ in / 4 cm. On last rnd, increase evenly spaced around to 39 (43, 43, 47, 51, 51)

Pattern A—Brown Pullover

repeat

repeat

center of sleeve

S L XXL

XS M XL

- V03 Light Gray Heather
- V13 Gray Heather
- V06 Beige Heather
- V55 Beige
- V64 Dark Brown Heather
- V14 Charcoal Gray Heather

Pattern A—Blue Pullover

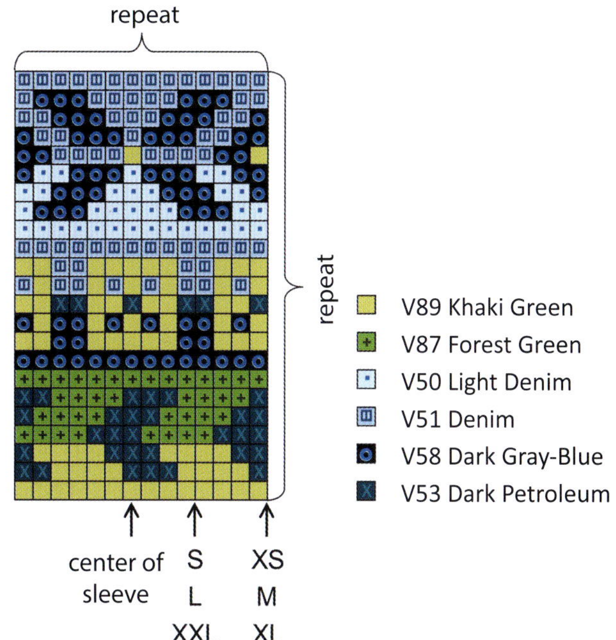

sts. Change to larger dpn and work around in Pattern A. Count out from center of sleeve to determine where to begin on chart. *At the same time*, increase 2 sts centered on underarm. Increase the same way every 1¼ (1¼, 1¼, 1¼, 1¼, 1¼) in / 3 (3, 3, 3, 3, 3) cm until there are 67 (71, 73, 77, 81, 81) sts. When sleeve is 19¼ (19¾, 20, 20, 20½, 20½) in / 49 (50, 51, 51, 52, 52) cm long, BO 6 (6, 8, 8, 10, 10) sts centered on underarm. Work back and forth and shape sleeve cap: at each side on every other row, BO 2,1,1 sts. Loosely BO rem sts.

FINISHING

Seam shoulders. Attach sleeves.

ROUND NECK

With MC and smaller circular, pick up and knit approx. 29 (29, 29, 31, 31, 31) sts along front neck, and 27 (27, 27, 29, 29, 29) sts along back neck. Join and work around in k1, p1 ribbing for 3¼ in / 8 cm. BO loosely in ribbing. Fold neckband double and sew down edge on WS.

V-NECK

With MC and smaller circular, beginning at center front, pick up and knit approx. 39 (41, 43, 45, 47, 47) sts along each side of front neck, and 27 (27, 27, 29, 29, 29) sts along back neck. Work back and forth in k1, p1 ribbing for 1¼ in / 3 cm. BO loosely in ribbing. Overlap one end over the other at center front and sew down invisibly.

Weave in all ends neatly on WS.

Dress with Fine Stripes

Let me present a striped dress without stripes. If you squint, they're there, but the eyes can easily be fooled!

Design: Marie Cecilie Dahl
Photos: Hilde Kvivik Kavli

PROJECT SUMMARY

- Slightly fitted dress with short sleeves
- Worked from the bottom up
- Stockinette pattern with garter stitch edges
- The body is knitted in the round; stitches are bound off for the underarms and then the front and back are worked separately, back and forth
- The sleeves are worked in the round up to the underarms, and then a short facing is worked back and forth; the finished sleeves are sewn into the armholes

SKILL LEVEL

Experienced

SIZES

S (M, L, XL, XXL)

FINISHED MEASUREMENTS

Chest: 36¼ (38¼, 40¼, 43¾, 45¼) in / 92 (97, 102, 111, 115) cm

Total Length: 32 (32¾, 33½, 34¼, 35) in / 81 (83, 85, 87, 89) cm

Sleeve Length: 8¼ (8¼, 8¾, 9, 9½) in / 21 (21, 22, 23, 24) cm

MATERIALS

Yarn: CYCA #2 (sport, baby) Rauma Finull (100% Norwegian wool, 191 yd/175 m / 50 g)

Yarn Colors and Amounts:
Light Powder Pink 4206: 200 (200, 250, 250, 300) g
Moss Green 476: 200 (200, 250, 300, 350) g
Jade Green 4215: 150 (150, 150, 200, 200) g

Needles: U. S. sizes 1.5 and 2.5 / 2.5 and 3 mm: circulars and sets of 5 dpn

GAUGE

26 sts in stockinette pattern on larger needles = 4 in / 10 cm in width.
Adjust needle sizes to obtain correct gauge if necessary.

BODY

With Moss Green and smaller circular, CO 276 (288, 300, 324, 336) sts. Join, being careful not to twist cast-on row. Pm for beginning of rnd and at side = 138 (144, 150, 162, 168) sts each for front and back. Work around in garter ridges for ¾ in / 2 cm (1 ridge = purl 1 rnd, knit 1 rnd).

Change to larger circular. Work following chart for Pattern A until body measures 7½ (8, 8¼ 8¾, 9) in / 19 (20, 21, 22, 23) cm. Decrease 2 sts at each side marker as follows: Knit until 3 sts before marker, k2tog tbl, k2, k2tog = 4 sts decreased on rnd. Decrease the same way every 1¾ in / 4.5 cm a total of 9 times = 240 (252, 264, 288, 300) sts rem, or 120 (126, 132, 144, 150) sts each for front and back.

When body measures 24¾ (25¼, 25½, 26, 26½) in / 63 (64, 65, 66, 67) cm, BO 12 (12, 12, 16, 16) sts centered over each side marker for underarms. CO 4 sts over each gap for steek. Always purl steek sts with Powder Pink. Steek sts are not included in stitch counts or pat-

counts or pattern. Continue working in the rnd.

At each armhole on front and back, on every other rnd, shape armholes by decreasing as follows: Knit until 2 sts before steek, k2tog tbl, purl steek sts, k2 tog. Decrease the same way a total of 6 (6, 6, 7, 7) times = 96 (102, 108, 114, 120) sts rem on each side (not counting steek).

When armhole depth is 6 (6¼, 6¾, 7, 7½) in / 15 (16, 17, 18, 19) cm, BO 50 (52, 54, 54, 56) sts centered on front for neck. Now work back and forth.

At beginning and end of row, on every other row, shape front neck: BO 3 sts once and 2 sts once. When armhole measures 6¼ (6¾, 7, 7½, 8) in / 16 (17, 18, 19, 20) cm, BO 54 (56, 58, 58, 60) sts centered on back for back neck and work each side separately. Continue, shaping back neck as follows: BO 3 sts once = 18 (20, 22, 25, 27) sts rem for shoulder. When armhole measures 6¾ (7, 7½, 8, 8¼) in 17 (18, 19, 20 , 21) cm, BO steek sts. Place rem front and back sts on holders. Work neckband back and forth, separately for front and back.

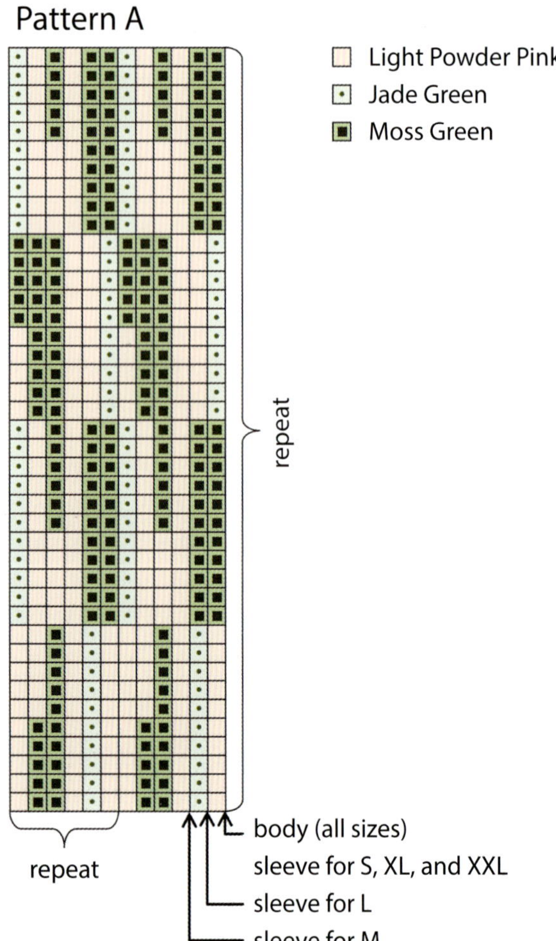

NECKBAND, FRONT

With Moss Green and smaller circular, pick up and knit sts in those bound off for front neck, about 1 st in each st. Slide held sts onto needle. Work back and forth in garter st (knit every row) for ⅜ in / 1 cm. On next row, place shoulder sts on each side on holders. BO rem sts.

NECKBAND, BACK

Work as for front neck.

SLEEVES

Make both alike. With Moss Green and smaller dpn, CO 78 (82, 86, 90, 96) sts. Divide sts onto dpn and join. Work around in garter st for ⅜ in / 1 cm. Change to larger dpn. Work following chart for Pattern A, beginning at arrow for your size. *At the same time*, increase 2 sts centered on underarm every ⅜ in / 1.5 cm a total of 9 (9, 9, 10, 10) times = 96 (100, 104, 110, 116) sts. When sleeve is 7½ (7½, 8, 8, 8¼) in / 19 (19, 20, 20, 21) cm long, BO the center 12 (12, 12, 16, 16) sts on underarm. Now work back and forth. Continue as est until sleeve is 8¼ (8¼, 8¾, 9, 9½) in / 21 (21, 22, 23, 24) cm long. Change to smaller circular. With WS facing, work 6 rows back and forth in stockinette for facing, increasing 1 st at each side on every row. BO loosely.

FINISHING

Machine-stitch 2 fine lines on each side of center steek sts. Carefully cut steek open up center between stitching lines. Join shoulders with Kitchener st or mattress st. Attach sleeves. Fold facings over cut edges and sew down invisibly so it won't show on RS. Weave in all ends neatly on WS.

Smart Colors on Round-Necked Pullover

Sometimes colors do things their own way and behave totally differently than you had envisioned. It is as if they change personality. In this instance, a flock of extrovert colors combine to create an almost low-key harmony.

Design: Rauma Garn / Stina Fredriksson
Photos: Pudder Agency / Julie Pike

PROJECT SUMMARY

- Pullover with round yoke
- Stockinette pattern with ribbing at lower edges of body and sleeves, and around neck
- Worked from the bottom up
- Body and sleeves worked separately to the underarms; then all the pieces are arranged on a circular, so the yoke can be worked in the round

SKILL LEVEL

Experience

SIZES

XS (S, M, L, XL, XXL)

FINISHED MEASUREMENTS

Chest: 34¾ (37, 40¼, 43, 46, 48¾) in / 88 (94, 102, 109, 117, 124) cm
Total Length: 24 (24¾, 25½, 26½, 26 ¾, 27¼) in / 61 (63, 65, 67, 68, 69) cm
Sleeve Length: 18½ (18½, 19, 19, 19¼, 19¼) in / 47 (47, 48, 48, 49, 49) cm

MATERIALS

Yarn: CYCA #2 (sport, baby) Rauma Finull (100% Norwegian wool, 191 yd/175 m / 50 g)

Yarn Colors and Amounts:
Gray-Beige 452: 300 (350, 400, 450, 500, 550) g
Old Rose 4571: 50 (50, 50, 50, 50, 50) g
Dark Gray-Blue 4387: 50 (50, 50, 50, 50, 50) g
Mustard Yellow 4805: 50 (50, 50, 50, 50, 50) g
Dark Denim 443: 50 (50, 50, 50, 50, 50) g

Needles: U. S. sizes 1.5 and 2.5 / 2.5 and 3 mm: circulars and sets of 5 dpn

GAUGE

26 sts in stockinette pattern on larger needles = 4 in / 10 cm in width.
NOTE: If you knit more tightly in two-color stranded knitting than in a single color, go up a needle size for the stranded colorwork.
Adjust needle sizes to obtain correct gauge if necessary

BODY

With Gray-Beige and smaller circular, CO 228 (244, 264, 284, 304, 320) sts. Join, being careful not to twist cast-on row. Pm for beginning of rnd and at side = 114 (122, 132, 142, 152, 160) sts each for front and back. Work around in k2, p2 ribbing for 2½ in / 6 cm. Change to larger circular and stockinette. When body measures 15¾ (16¼, 16½, 17, 17, 17) in / 40 (41, 42, 43, 43, 43) cm, BO 8 (8, 10, 10, 12, 12) sts centered at each side

for underarms = 106 (114, 122, 132, 140, 148) sts rem each for front and back. Set body aside while you knit sleeves.

SLEEVES

Make both alike. With Gray-Beige and smaller dpn, CO 64 (64, 68, 68, 72, 72) sts. Divide sts onto dpn and join. Work around in k2, p2 ribbing for 2½ in / 6 cm. Change to larger dpn and stockinette. *At the same time*, increase 2 sts centered on underarm approx. every 1½ (1¼, 1¼, 1, 1, ¾) in / 4 (3, 3, 2.5, 2.5, 2) cm a total of 10 (12, 13, 15, 16, 18) times = 84 (88, 94, 98, 104, 108) sts. When sleeve is 18½ (18½, 19, 19, 19¼, 19¼) in / 47 (47, 48, 48, 49, 49) cm long, BO 8 (8, 10, 10, 12, 12) sts centered on underarm = 76 (80, 84, 88, 92, 96) sts rem.

YOKE

Arrange body and sleeves on long, larger circular, matching underarms = 364 (388, 412, 440, 464, 488) sts total. Pm at each intersection of sleeve and body = 4 markers. Continue in stockinette with Gray-Beige. On next rnd, begin raglan decreasing at all 4 markers as follows: Work until 3 sts before first marker, k2tog tbl, k2, k2tog. Decrease the same way at each marker = 8 sts decreased around. Decrease the same way on every other rnd a total of 3 (3, 4, 4, 5, 5) times = 340 (364, 380, 408, 424, 448) sts rem. Knit 1 rnd, *at the same time*, decreasing 25 (34, 35, 48, 49, 58) sts evenly spaced around = 315 (330, 345, 360, 375, 390) sts rem. Work following chart for Pattern A, decreasing as indicated on chart. At arrow for neck, place 73 (77, 80, 84, 87, 91) sts at center front on a holder for neck. Work back and forth over rem sts.

Raise back with short rows: Beginning on RS, work until 4 sts rem; turn, work back until 4 sts rem; turn. Work until 8 sts rem on needle; turn and work until 8 sts rem; turn. Work until 12 sts rem on needle; turn and work until 12 sts rem. Work until 16 sts rem on needle; turn and work until 16 sts rem. Work until 20 sts rem on needle; turn and work until 20 sts rem.

Knit 1 rnd with Gray-Beige over all sts, and *at the same time* decrease 3 (6, 13, 16, 23, 26) sts evenly spaced around = 144 (148, 148, 152, 152,156) sts

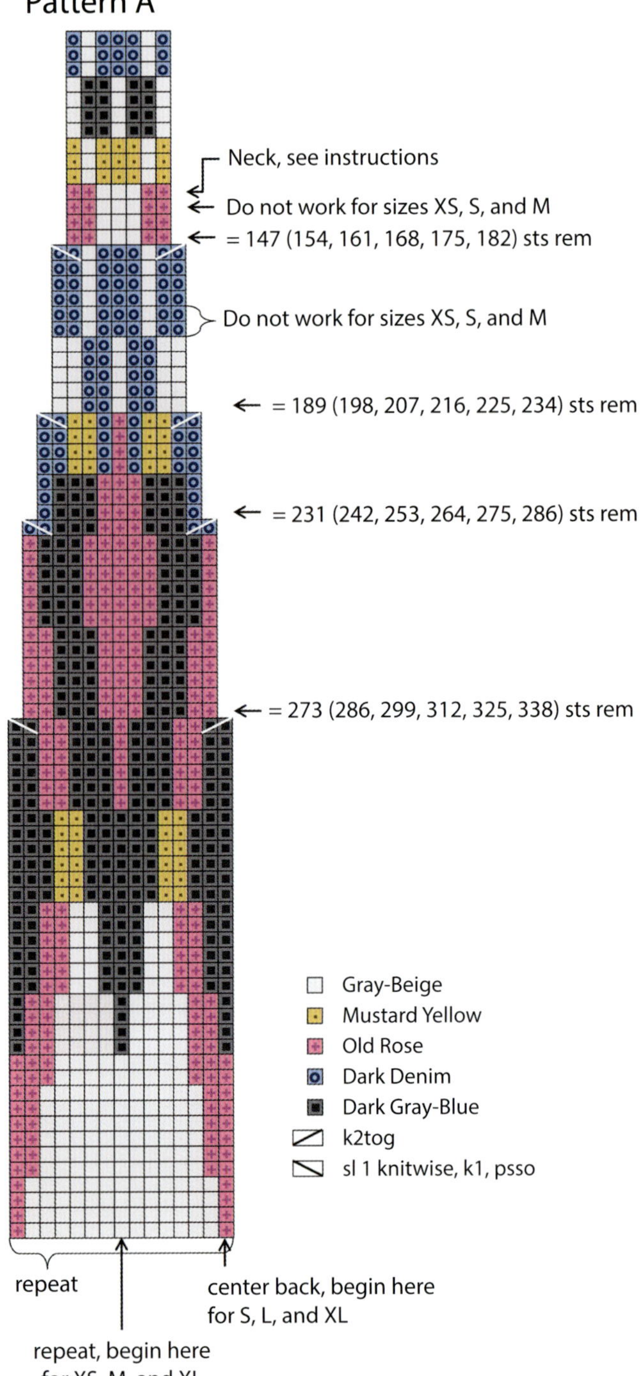

rem. Change to smaller circular. With Gray-Beige, work around in k2, p2 ribbing for 8 in / 20 cm. BO in ribbing.

FINISHING

Seam underarms. Weave in all ends neatly on WS.

GEMS FROM THE ARCHIVE

Pattern No. 228: Women's Cardigan

We'll go back a few years, back to the time when charts were hand-drawn; in Norwegian, the word for them (*plansjer*) translates literally as "plates." A very abbreviated pattern leaves almost everything to the knitter's imagination—possibly because everyone at that time already knew exactly what a Norwegian sweater should look like, and how it should be knitted.

PROJECT SUMMARY

- Cardigan with sewn-in sleeves
- Ribbing at lower edges of body and sleeves, stockinette on front bands and neckband
- Worked from the bottom up
- The body is worked in the round with a center front steek, and the front and armholes are cut open later
- The sleeves are knit in the round, bound off for a straight cap, and sewn into the armholes
- The front bands are worked separately and sewn onto the front opening

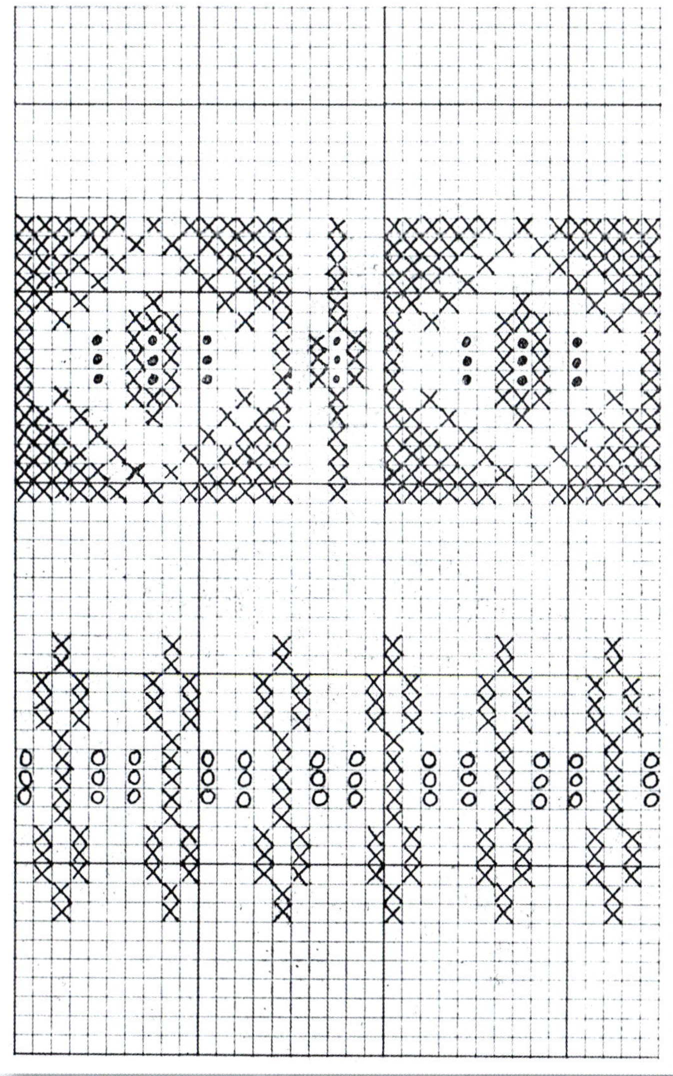

☐ No. 116 Sheep's Brown
☒ No. 101 Bleached White
◙ No. 115 Yellow
▣ No. 168 Blue

Pattern No. 228: Women's Cardigan

With Rauma Yarn, size 42

SKILL LEVEL

Experienced

SIZES

Women's 42

MATERIALS

Yarn: CYCA # 3 (DK, light worsted) Rauma 3-ply Strikkegarn (100% Norwegian wool, 118 yd/108 m / 50 g)

Yarn Colors and Amounts:
Brown 116: 5 balls
Bleached White 101: 2 balls
Yellow 115: ¼ ball
Blue 168: ¼ ball

Needles: U. S. sizes 1.5 and 2.5 / 2.5 and 3 mm: circulars and sets of 5 dpn

GAUGE

22 sts in stockinette pattern on larger needles = 4 in / 10 cm in width.
Adjust needle sizes to obtain correct gauge if necessary.

BODY

With smaller circular, CO 220 sts. Work in k2, p2 ribbing for 3¼ in / 8 cm. Change to larger circular and increase evenly spaced around to 260 sts. Work in pattern as shown on chart. Join shoulders.

SLEEVES

With smaller dpn, CO 48 sts. Work in k2, p2 ribbing for 3¼ in / 8 cm. Change to larger dpn and increase evenly spaced around to 64 sts. Work in pattern as shown on chart and increase to 116 sts, with increases evenly spaced up sleeve. Finish with Brown for 5 rnds for facing.

FRONT BANDS

CO 10 sts. Work back and forth in garter stitch. For each buttonhole, BO 3 sts on one row and CO 3 sts over gap on following row.

NECKBAND

Work neckband after front bands have been sewn on. Pick up and knit 94 sts and work in stockinette for 1¼ in / 3 cm.

FINISHING

With fine stitches, machine-stitch two rows up front and cut open. Sew on bands by machine, right side facing right side, fold over and sew down by hand on wrong side.

Attach sleeves by machine and sew facing over cut edges of armhole on wrong side.

Kitchener Stitch Join

This drawing shows how to join the shoulders. The stitches must align with the rest of the pattern. The joining won't always be positioned on a single-color row, and in that case, you may have to use multiple colors of yarn. Use a tapestry needle and yarn from the cardigan to "sew" the stitches together. Follow the arrows as shown on the drawing and make sure the tension of the Kitchener stitches matches the knitted stitches. Fasten off yarn well.

KNITTING FOLLOWING THE PATTERN INSTRUCTIONS

Most patterns are sized for "average" knitting, insofar as that can be approximated. But not everyone knits at the same gauge. To make sure your garment will be the correct size, we recommend knitting a gauge swatch. Cast on 20 sts and work 20 rows. Count how many stitches are in 4 inches / 10 cm, and then calculate the sizing from there.

WASHING KNITTED GARMENTS

Use lukewarm water and mild soap. For wool yarn, the washing water should not be warmer than your hands can tolerate. Press the water into the garment. Do not twist or wring the garment. Rinse several times in same temperature water as for the soap wash. Pat garment into shape and lay flat to dry on a damp towel, preferably on a pile of old newspapers, which will function like blotting paper.

A GOOD KNITTING TIP

Always knit the sleeves first. After that, you can better calculate the size of the garment. You'll also be more familiar with the pattern motifs.

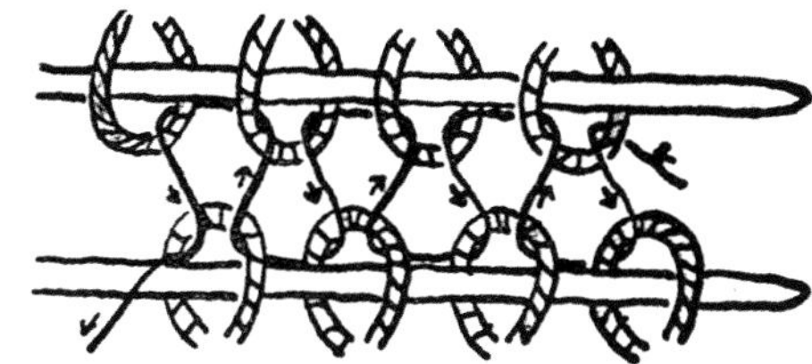

Cabled Favorites and Textures for Every Day

For some knitters, cable or texture patterns are intimidating. The result looks so complicated that people think there must be magic somewhere in the picture, at the very least. It probably doesn't help when experienced cablers claim that it's actually easy.

Sure, you think, of course it is, when we already know how to do it. Listen, the only things you need to learn, which you can just google, are:

1. How to use a cable needle.
2. How to make a yarnover.
3. How to knit stitches together.

Other than that, it only requires stitches you're probably already familiar with—knit and purl, and so on. The techniques are described in the pattern instructions. Skeptical? Just check it out—and remember that it actually is as easy as I say. In which case, you only have three steps between you and a magic world of cables and textured knitting!

Cozy Vest with Leaf Patterns

If you're one of those people who like the feeling of wool next to your skin, this vest will be a good friend and keep you dry and cool—it both warms and breathes. And it's also so pretty and delicate. . .!

Design: Rauma Garn / Ane Tyssøy Godal
Photos: Hilde Kvivik Kavli

PROJECT SUMMARY

- V-neck vest
- Ribbing around lower edges of body and neck; lace yoke
- Worked from the bottom up
- Body is worked in the round to the underarms; then the body is divided into back and front and each is worked separately, back and forth

SKILL LEVEL

Intermediate/Experienced

SIZES

XS/S (S/M, L/XL)

FINISHED MEASUREMENTS

Chest: approx. 28¼ (31½, 34¾) in / 72 (80, 88) cm
Total Length: approx. 21¾ (22½, 23¼) in / 55 (57, 59) cm

MATERIALS

Yarn: CYCA # 1 (light fingering) Rauma Lamullgarn (100% Norwegian wool, 273 yd/250 m / 50 g)

Yarn Colors and Amounts:
Natural L11: 100 (150, 150) g

Needles: U. S. sizes 1.5 / 2.5 mm: circular

GAUGE

30 sts in pattern = 4 in / 10 cm in width.
Adjust needle sizes to obtain correct gauge if necessary.

BODY

With circular, CO 216 (240, 264) sts. Join, being careful not to twist cast-on row; pm for beginning of rnd. Work around in p1, k1 ribbing for 10¾ in / 27 cm and then in lace pattern for 2½ (2¾, 3¼) in / 6 (7, 8) cm.
Next Rnd: Work 18 sts p1, k1 ribbing (= half of one armhole edge), lace pattern over 30 (36, 42) sts (= one half front), 13 sts k1, p1 ribbing (= neck edge, center front), pattern over 30 (36, 42) sts (= second half of front), 35 sts k1, p1 ribbing (second armhole edge), pattern over 73 (85, 97) sts (= back), 17 sts k1, p1 ribbing (half armhole edge).
Continue as est for ¾ in / 2 cm.
Next Rnd: BO 23 sts on each side, centered on each armhole, for underarms = 85 (97, 109) sts rem each for front and back.

Now work each side separately.

FRONT

Work back and forth. Continue in ribbing as est over the outermost 6 sts at each side (= armhole edges) and the center 13 sts (= neck), and in lace pattern over rem sts.
At armhole edge, on every other row (on WS), k2tog inside armhole edge, 10 (16, 22) times. Work joined sts

as purl on RS rows. *At the same time*, when piece measures 14¼ (14½, 15) in / 36 (37, 38) cm, BO the center st on each side of front and work each side separately. Continue with ribbing and lace, and shape V-neck as follows (on WS rows): K2tog inside neck edge until 13 sts rem and neck and armhole edges meet. Work joined sts as purl on RS rows. Body now measures approx. 21¾ (22, 22½) in / 55 (56, 57) cm. Continue in ribbing until body measures 21¾ (22½, 23¼) in / 55 (57, 59) cm.

Place rem sts on a holder or BO.

Work opposite side to correspond.

BACK

Work back and forth. Continue in ribbing as est over the outermost 6 sts at each side (= armhole edges) and in lace pattern over rem sts. *At the same time*, shape armholes as for front = 65 sts (all sizes). When back is 2½ in / 6 cm shorter than front, work ribbing over all sts for 1¼ in / 3 cm.

Next Row: BO the center 39 sts for back neck = 13 sts rem for shoulder on each side.

Work each side separately. Continue with ribbing until back is same length as front. Place rem sts on a holder or BO.

FINISHING

Join shoulders with Kitchener st or mattress st.

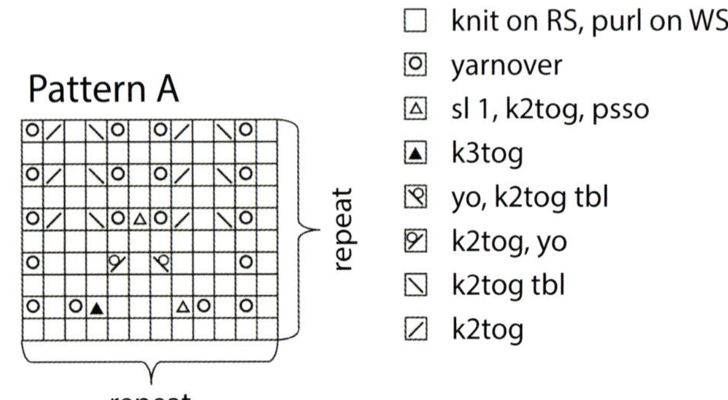

Violet Vest

… when the pattern looks like flower leaves—and fills your thoughts with summer warmth, sunshine, blue skies, and long, late days …

Design: Rauma Garn / Britt Kathrine Aasen
Photos: Siren Lauvdal

PROJECT SUMMARY

- Straight vest with V-neck vest and button closures
- Texture pattern—with garter ridges at lower edge, around armholes, and along front edges and neck
- Worked from the bottom up
- The front and back are worked back and forth in one piece to the underarms; then the body is divided into back and front and each is worked separately, back and forth
- The armhole and neck edges are worked last

SKILL LEVEL

Experienced

SIZES

XS (S, M, L, XL, XXL)

FINISHED MEASUREMENTS

Chest: (38¼, 40½, 43¼, 45¾, 50½) in / 91 (97, 103, 110, 116, 128) cm

Total Length: 28 (28¾, 29½, 30¼, 31, 32) in / 71 (73, 75, 77, 79, 81) cm

MATERIALS

Yarn: CYCA # 2 (sport, baby) Rauma Finull (100% Norwegian wool, 191 yd/175 m / 50 g)

Yarn Colors and Amounts:

Light Blue Heather 4139 or Heathery Heather 4126: 250 (250, 300, 300, 350, 350) g

Needles: U. S. sizes 1.5 and 2.5 / 2.5 and 3 mm: circulars; cable needle

Notions: 7-8 buttons

GAUGE

26 sts in pattern on larger needles = 4 in / 10 cm in width.
Adjust needle sizes to obtain correct gauge if necessary.

BODY—FRONT AND BACK IN ONE PIECE

With smaller circular, CO 237 (253, 269, 285, 301, 333) sts. Knit back and forth in garter st (knit all rows) for ¾ in / 2 cm. Change to larger circular. Pm at each side with 59 (63, 66, 71, 75, 83) sts for each front and 119 (127, 137, 143, 151, 167) sts for back. Now work following chart for Pattern A. When body measures 21 (21¼, 21¾, 22, 22½, 22¾) in / 53 (54, 55, 56, 57, 58) cm, BO 8 sts at each side (= 4 sts on each side of each marker) for underarms.
Now work back and front separately.

BACK

= 111 (119, 129, 135, 143, 159) sts.
Continue working back and forth in pattern. *At the same time*, shape armholes: on every other row, BO 2 sts once, 1 st once. When armhole depth measures 6½ (6¾, 7, 7½, 8, 8¼, 8¾) in / 16 (18, 19, 20, 21, 22) cm, place the center 39 (41, 45, 47, 49, 51) sts on a holder for back neck. Work each side separately. At neck edge, on every other row, BO 2 sts once and then 1 st once = 30 (33, 36, 38, 41, 48) sts rem for shoulder. When armhole depth measures 7 (7½, 8, 8¼, 8¾, 9) in / 18 (19, 20, 21, 22, 23) cm, BO rem sts.

FRONT

= 55 (59, 62, 67, 71, 79) sts.

Work and shape armholes as for back. *At the same time*, when armhole measures ¾ in / 2 cm, begin V-neck, decreasing inside 2 edge sts: Decrease 1 st on every other row 22 (23, 23, 26, 27, 28) times. After all neck and armhole decreases have been worked, 30 (33, 36, 38, 41, 48) sts rem for shoulder. When armhole depth measures 7 (7½, 8, 8¼, 8¾, 9) in / 18 (19, 20, 21, 22, 23) cm, BO rem sts.

FINISHING

Join shoulders.

FRONT BANDS

With smaller circular and RS facing, pick up and knit approx. 13 sts per 2 in / 5 cm along left front edge, knit the held back neck sts, and then pick up and knit sts along right front edge (same number of sts as for left front). Knit back and forth in garter ridges for approx. ¾ in / 2 cm, but after ⅜ in / 1 cm, make buttonholes down left front band.

Buttonhole spacing: Place top buttonhole at base of V-neck, lowest buttonhole ¾ in / 2 cm above lower edge; space 5-6 more buttonholes evenly between.

Buttonhole: BO 2 sts and, on next row, CO 2 sts over each gap.

Complete band and BO.

ARMHOLE EDGINGS

With smaller circular and RS facing, pick up and knit approx. 13 sts per 2 in / 5 cm around armhole edge. Knit around in garter sts (= alternate knit 1 rnd, purl 1 rnd) for ¾ in / 2 cm. BO.

Sew on buttons. Weave in all ends neatly on WS.

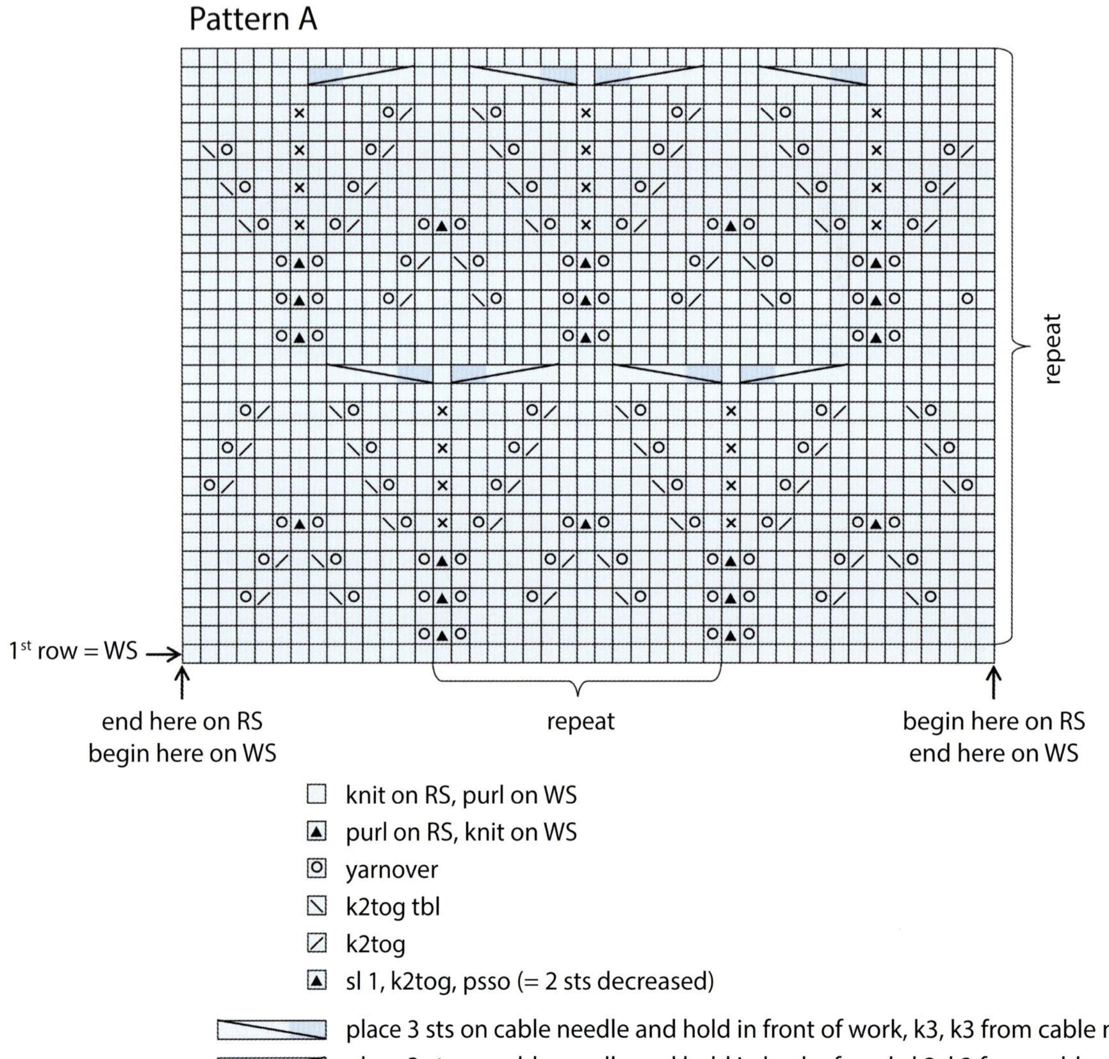

- knit on RS, purl on WS
- purl on RS, knit on WS
- yarnover
- k2tog tbl
- k2tog
- sl 1, k2tog, psso (= 2 sts decreased)
- place 3 sts on cable needle and hold in front of work, k3, k3 from cable needle
- place 3 sts on cable needle and hold in back of work, k3, k3 from cable needle

Must-Have Cardigan with Shawl Collar

I read somewhere that every basic wardrobe must have a cardigan in a warm, natural material. This is a garment that's handy for a cool office and late summer evenings after sundown. Perhaps it was precisely this sweater that I was reading about.

Design and Photos: Rauma Garn

PROJECT SUMMARY

- Cardigan with shawl collar and button closures
- Texture pattern or cable pattern as you wish
- Ribbing along lower edges of body and sleeves, as well as on front edges and around neck
- Worked from the bottom up
- The front and back are worked back and forth in one piece to the underarms; then, the body is divided into back and front and each is worked separately, back and forth
- The sleeves are worked in the round up to the underarms, and then a short sleeve cap is worked back and forth; the finished sleeves are sewn into the armholes
- The front edges and collar are worked last

SKILL LEVEL

Experienced

SIZES

XS (S, M, L, XL, XXL, 3XL)

FINISHED MEASUREMENTS

Chest: 37½ (40½, 43¾, 47, 50, 53¼, 56¼) in / 95 (103, 111, 119, 127, 135, 143) cm
Total Length: 24 (24½, 25¼, 26, 26¾, 27½, 28¼) in / 61 (62, 64, 66, 68, 70, 72) cm
Sleeve Length: 18¼ (18½, 19, 19¼, 19¾, 20, 20½) in / 46 (47, 48, 49, 50, 51, 52) cm

MATERIALS

Yarn: CYCA # 3 (DK, light worsted) Rauma 3-ply Strikkegarn (100% Norwegian wool, 118 yd/108 m / 50 g)

Yarn Colors and Amounts:
Light Peasant Blue 168 or Light Gray Heather 103: 550 (550, 650, 700, 750, 800, 850) g

Needles: U. S. sizes 2.5 and 4 / 3 and 3.5 mm: circulars and sets of 5 dpn; cable needle

Notions: 6-7 buttons

GAUGE

20 sts in pattern on larger needles = 4 in / 10 cm in width.
Adjust needle sizes to obtain correct gauge if necessary.

TURNING TIPS

After every turn, slip first st without knitting it.

BODY

The body is worked back and forth on a circular needle.
With smaller circular, CO 181 (197, 213, 229, 245, 261, 277) sts. Work back and forth in k1, p1 ribbing for 2½ (2½, 2½, 2¾, 2¾, 2¾, 2¾) in / 6 (6, 6, 7, 7, 7, 7) cm, ending with a WS row. Pm on the 43rd (47th, 51st, 55th, 59th, 63rd, 67th) st and the 139th (151st, 163rd, 175th, 187th, 199th, 211th) st = side markers. Change to larger circular. Now work following chart for Pattern A.
NOTE: The first and last sts are edge sts and always knitted throughout.

When body measures 14¼ (14¼, 14½, 15, 15½, 15¾, 16¼) in / 36 (36, 37, 38, 39, 40, 41) cm, decrease 1 st inside edge st at beginning and end of row for V-neck. Decrease the same way every 6th (6th, 6th, 4th, 4th, 4th, 4th) row. *At the same time*, when body measures 16¼ (16¼, 16½, 17, 17¾, 18¼, 18½) in / 41 (41, 42, 43, 45, 46, 47) cm, BO 7 sts at each side (= marked st + 3 sts on each side marked st) for underarms. Now work back and front separately.

BACK

= 89 (97, 105, 113, 121, 129, 137) sts.

Work back and forth in pattern as est. Shape armholes at each side, on every other row: decrease 1 st 6 times = 77 (85, 93, 101, 109, 117, 125) sts rem. When body measures 23¼ (23¾, 24½, 25¼, 25½, 26¾, 27½) in / 59 (60, 62, 64, 65, 68, 70) cm, BO the center 23 (25, 27, 29, 31, 33, 35 sts for back neck. Work each side separately. At neck edge, on every other row, BO 2 sts once and then 1 st once = 24 (27, 30, 33, 36, 39, 42) sts rem for shoulder. When body measures 24 (24½, 25¼, 26, 26¾, 27½, 28¼) in / 61 (62, 64, 66, 68, 70, 72) cm, BO rem sts.

FRONT

Continue neck shaping as est and, *at the same time*, shape armholes as for back. When 24 (27, 30, 33, 36, 39, 42) sts rem for shoulder, neck shaping is complete. Work as est until front is same length as back and then BO rem sts.

SLEEVES

Make both alike. The sleeves are worked in the round. With smaller dpn, CO 44 (46, 48, 50, 50, 52, 54) sts. Divide sts onto dpn and join. Work around in k1, p1 ribbing for 2½ (2½, 2½, 2¾, 2¾, 2¾, 2¾) in / 6 (6, 6, 7, 7, 7, 7) cm. On last rnd, increase 8 sts evenly spaced around = 52 (54, 56, 58, 58, 60, 62) sts. Change to larger dpn. Pm in 1st st (= center of underarm); always purl this marked st. Work following chart for pattern. Begin by counting out from center of sleeve to determine where to begin on chart. Shape sleeve by increasing 2 sts centered on underarm (increase 1 on each side of purl st) every ¾ in / 2 cm 14 (15, 16, 17, 17, 18, 19) times = 80 (84, 88, 92, 92, 96, 100) sts. When sleeve is 18¼ (18½, 19, 19¼, 19¾, 20, 20½) in / 46 (47, 48, 49, 50, 51, 52) cm long, BO first (purl) st and work back and forth. *At the same time*, on every other row, BO 3 sts once and then 1 st 5 times. Work 1 rnd after last decrease. BO rem sts.

FINISHING

Join shoulders with Kitchener st or mattress st.

FRONT BANDS AND COLLAR

Place 5 markers as follows: at center back neck, on each shoulder seam, on each front at base of V-neck. With smaller circular, beginning at lower edge of right front, pick up and knit approx. 22 sts per 4 in / 10 cm along right front, around neck, and down left front. Make sure there are the same number of sts on each half of the sweater, with the same number of sts on each side below V-neck, the same number of sts along V-neck to shoulder, and the same number of sts on each side of shoulder to marker at center back.

Work 1 row of k1, p1 ribbing over all sts. On the next row, work past the first shoulder marker and another 4 sts past the second shoulder marker. Turn (see Turning Tips on page 98) and work back until 4 sts past first shoulder marker. Turn, and work 8 sts past second shoulder marker. Continue the same way by turning and working 4 more sts on each side each time until all the sts above the V-neck are included. Now work 10 rows over all sts, completely up/down each side of front. On the 5th row, make 6-7 buttonholes, on the right front for women and left front for men.

Buttonhole Spacing: Place bottom buttonhole ⅜ in / 1 cm above lower edge and top buttonhole ⅜ in / 1 cm below base of V-neck; space 4-6 more buttonholes evenly between.

Buttonhole: BO 2 sts and, on next row, CO 2 sts over each gap.

Complete the 10 rows of band and BO a bit firmly. However, make sure BO is not too tight across back neck.

Attach sleeves. Sew on buttons. Weave in all ends neatly on WS. The collar can stand up on back neck or be folded down.

Pattern A—Women's Cardigan

repeat

repeat

center of sleeve

begin here for body

knit on RS, purl on WS

purl on RS, knit on WS

brioche: k1 into st below first st on left needle

yarnover, slip 1, k2tog, psso, yo

Pattern A—Men's Cardigan

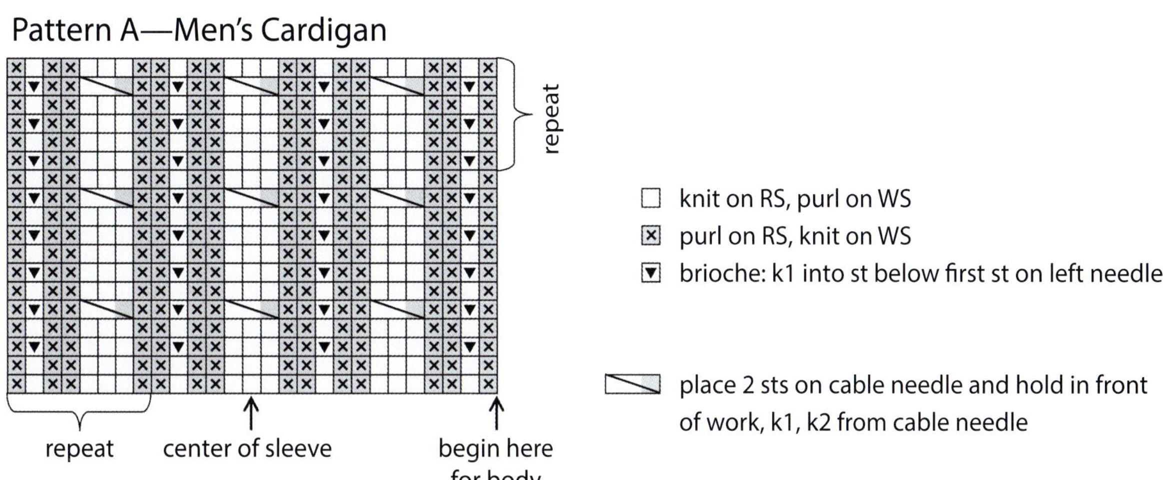

Men's Pullover with Shifting Cables

How is it possible? This pattern needs a closer look. It might appear amazingly complicated, but it's actually a simple combination of cables and purl sections that shift.

Design: Rauma Garn
Photos: Elisabeth Tollisen

PROJECT SUMMARY

- Pullover with a square neck opening and shawl collar
- Cable and texture pattern with ribbing at lower edges of body and sleeves, and around neck
- Worked from the bottom up
- Front, back, and sleeves each worked separately, back and forth
- All pieces are sewn together
- The collar is worked last, back and forth

SKILL LEVEL

Experienced

SIZES

S (M, L, XL)

FINISHED MEASUREMENTS

Chest: 36¾ (40¼, 45, 48¾) in / 93 (102, 114, 124) cm
Total Length: 27½ (28¼, 29¼, 30) in / 70 (72, 74, 76) cm
Sleeve Length: 19¼ (19¾, 20½, 21¼) in / 49 (50, 52, 54) cm

MATERIALS

Yarn: CYCA #5 (bulky) Rauma Vams PT3 (100% Norwegian wool, 90 yd/83 m / 50 g)

Yarn Colors and Amounts:
Petroleum V47: 700 (750, 800, 850) g

Needles: U. S. sizes 7 and 8 / 4.5 and 5 mm: circulars and straights or circular for sleeves; cable needle

GAUGE

17 sts in pattern on larger needles = 4 in / 10 cm in width.
Adjust needle sizes to obtain correct gauge if necessary.

BACK

With smaller circular, CO 80 (88, 98, 106) sts. Work back and forth in k2, p2 ribbing for 2½ in / 6 cm. Change to larger circular. Work following chart for Pattern A, beginning at arrow for your size. On the sizes where the blocks with cables don't have enough stitches to work the cable, knit sts instead of working cable (at the beginning and end of the row). Continue in pattern until back measures 27½ (28¼, 29¼, 30) in / 70 (72, 74, 76) cm. BO all sts or place sts on a holder.

FRONT

Work as for back until piece measures 19¾ (20, 20½, 21) in / 50 (51, 52, 53) cm. BO 30 sts centered on front for front neck = 25 (29, 34, 38) sts rem on each side of front. Work each side separately. Continue in pattern as for back until front measures 27½ (28¼, 29¼, 30) in / 70 (72, 74, 76) cm. BO all sts or place sts on a holder.

SLEEVES

With smaller needles, CO 44 (48, 48, 52) sts. Work back and forth in k2, p2 ribbing for 2½ in / 6 cm. On last row, increase 4 (4, 6, 4) sts evenly spaced across = 48 (52, 54, 56) sts. Change to larger needles. Work following chart for Pattern B. Count out from center of sleeve to determine where to begin pattern on chart. *At the same time*, increase 2 sts centered on underarm every 6th row a total of 15 (15, 16, 16) times = 78 (82, 86, 88) sts. BO all sts when sleeve is 19¼ (19¾, 20½, 21¼) in / 49 (50, 52, 54) cm long.

FINISHING

Join shoulders with Kitchener st or mattress st. Attach sleeves. Sew sleeves and sides as one seam.

NECKBAND

With RS facing, begin band at lower right corner of front neck opening. With smaller circular, pick up and knit approx. 10 sts per 2 in / 5 cm all around neck, down to left corner. Work back and forth in k2, p2 ribbing until band is as wide as the bound-off opening. BO 10 sts at each side of row and then BO 8 sts on every other row 5 times. BO rem sts in ribbing.
Overlap ends at center front and sew down collar.

Weave in all ends neatly on WS.

Pattern A

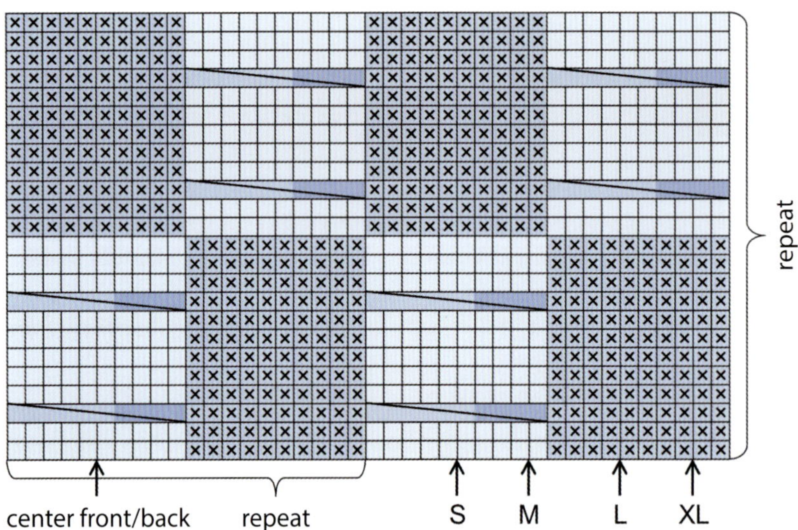

Pattern B

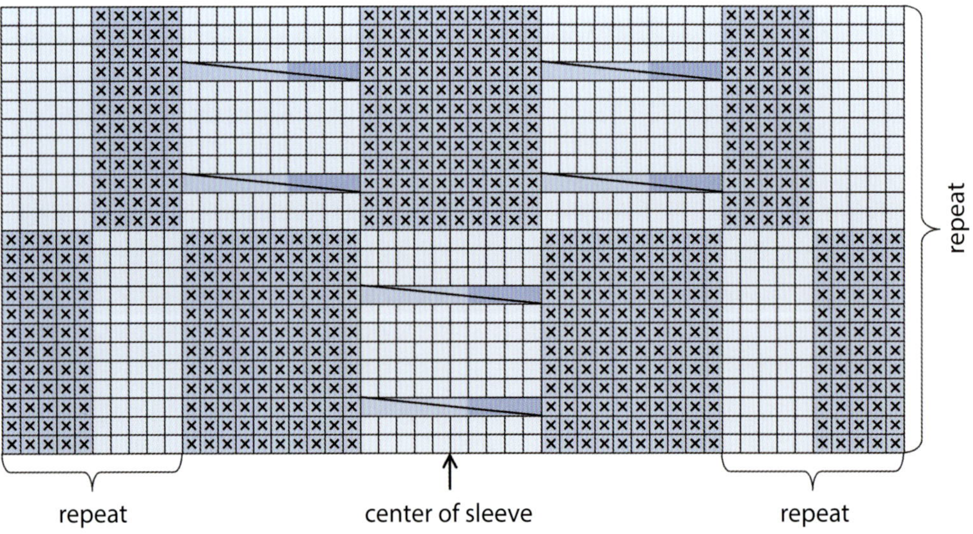

- knit on RS, purl on WS
- purl on RS, knit on WS
- place 5 sts on cable needle and hold in front of work, k5, k5 from cable needle

73

Titan Cabled Pullover

A sturdy companion for slit jeans—or a sweet, flowery summer dress, which is my personal preference. Really, though, it goes with almost anything. A pullover after my own heart!

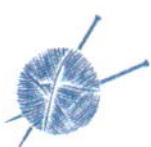

Design: Rauma Garn / Ber-Lin Design
Photos: Siren Lauvdal

PROJECT SUMMARY

- V-neck pullover
- Cables around the body and centered on the sleeves, with ribbing at lower edges of body and sleeves, and around neck
- Worked from the bottom up
- The body is worked in the round up to the neck opening, and then worked back and forth; it's then divided at the underarms, and front and back are worked separately, back and forth
- The sleeves are worked in the round all the way up, and then bound off straight across and sewn into armholes
- The neckband is worked last

SKILL LEVEL

Experienced

SIZES

XS (S, M, L, XL, XXL)

FINISHED MEASUREMENTS

Chest: 37 (39½, 43¾, 47¼, 49¾, 51½) in / 94 (100, 111, 120, 126, 131) cm
Total Length: 19¾ (20½, 21¼, 22, 22¾, 23¾) in / 50 (52, 54, 56, 58, 60) cm
Sleeve Length: 18½ (19, 19, 19¼, 19¼, 19¾) in / 47 (48, 48, 49, 49, 50) cm

MATERIALS

Yarn: CYCA #5 (bulky) Rauma Vams PT3 (100% Norwegian wool, 90 yd/83 m / 50 g)

Yarn Colors and Amounts:
Light Gray Heather V03: 500 (550, 600, 650, 700, 750) g

Needles: U. S. sizes 8 and 10 / 5 and 6 mm: circulars and sets of 5 dpn; cable needle

GAUGE

14 sts in stockinette on larger needles = 4 in / 10 cm in width.
Adjust needle sizes to obtain correct gauge if necessary.

BODY

With smaller circular, CO 132 (140, 156, 168, 176, 184) sts. Join, being careful not to twist cast-on row. Pm for beginning of rnd and side = 66 (70, 78, 84, 88, 92) sts each for front and back. Work around in k2, p2 ribbing for 1½ (1½, 1½, 2, 2, 2) in / 4 (4, 4, 5, 5, 5) cm. Change to larger circular. Knit 1 rnd, *at the same time* increasing 34 sts evenly spaced over the center 56 sts each of front and back = 200 (208, 224, 236, 244, 252) sts. On next rnd, set up pattern as follows: K5 (7, 11, 14, 16, 18), work following chart for pattern over next 90 sts, k5 (7, 11, 14, 16, 18) = front. Work back the same way. Continue as est until body measures approx. 11¾ (12¾, 12¾, 13½, 13¾, 14½) in / 30 (32, 32, 34, 35, 37) cm. (See below for concurrent measurements on larger sizes for beginning underarms.) BO 2 sts centered on front for base of V-neck. Beginning at center front, work back and forth. Continue shaping V-neck: on every other row, decrease 1 st at each side of neck. *At the same time*, when body measures approx. 12¼ (12¾, 13, 13½, 13¾, 14½) in / 31 (32, 33, 34, 35, 37) cm, divide body at each side. Work front and back separately.

BACK

Continue working back and forth as est until back measures approx. 19¾ (20½, 21¼, 22, 22¾, 23¾) in / 50 (52, 54, 56, 58, 60) cm. BO 34 sts evenly spaced across the center 90 sts (to 56 sts) = 66 (70, 78, 84, 88, 92) sts rem. BO rem sts.

FRONT

Work back and forth and continue to shape V-neck as est until you've decreased a total of 7 (7, 7, 7, 8, 8) times. Now decrease on every 4th row 9 (9, 10, 10, 10, 10) times. When front is same length as back, BO rem sts.

SLEEVES

Make both alike. With smaller dpn, CO 28 (28, 28, 32, 32, 32) sts. Divide sts onto dpn and join. Work around in k2, p2 ribbing for 2 (2, 2, 2½, 2½, 2½) in / 5 (5, 5, 6, 6, 6) cm. On the last rnd, increase evenly spaced around to 44 (48, 52, 52, 56, 56) sts. Change to larger dpn. On next rnd, set up pattern as follows: K10 (12, 14, 14, 16, 16), work following chart for pattern over next 24 sts, k10 (12, 14, 14, 16, 16). Continue as est, and *at the same time* increase 2 sts centered on underarm every 1½ in / 4 cm a total of 10 (9, 9, 10, 9, 10) times = 64 (66, 70, 72, 74, 76) sts. When sleeve is 18½ (19, 19, 19¼, 19¼, 19¾) in / 47 (48, 48, 49, 49, 50) cm long, BO 10 sts evenly spaced over cable at center of sleeve = 54 (56, 60, 62, 64, 66) sts rem. BO rem sts.

FINISHING

Join shoulders. Attach sleeves.

NECKBAND

With RS facing and with smaller circular, pick up and knit sts, beginning at right shoulder. Pick up and knit about 7 sts per 2 in / 5 cm along back neck, down V-neck, and up to beginning of rnd = approx. 92 (92, 100, 100, 108, 108) sts; the stitch count must be a multiple of 4. Pm at beginning of rnd. Work around in k2, p2 ribbing. Pm at center front, at V-neck between either 2 knit or 2 purl sts. Decrease 1 st on each side of marker on every other rnd. Continue as est until neckband measures approx. 2 in / 5 cm. BO in ribbing.

Weave in all ends neatly on WS.

Pattern

repeat

end here

work 4 times on front and back, and once on sleeves

begin here

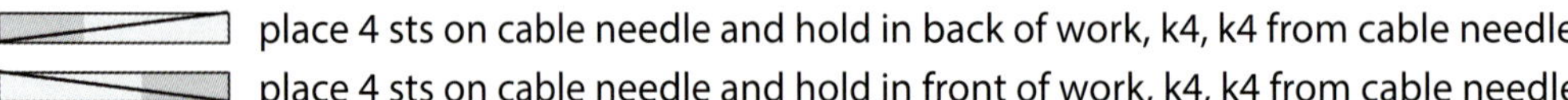

☐ knit on RS, purl on WS

☒ purl on RS, knit on WS

place 4 sts on cable needle and hold in back of work, k4, k4 from cable needle

place 4 sts on cable needle and hold in front of work, k4, k4 from cable needle

GEMS FROM THE ARCHIVE

4001 Cardigan with Hood

Less is more. I've heard experts on various subjects say this, and give many reasons why it's true. But wait—sometimes it can be nice to just pile it on, isn't that so? And here, so much is happening! What if we go back to the 1980s, when clothes spoke with large, lush letters? Cables, texture, and moss stitches all over, small and large bobbles, ribbing, hoods, shoulder pieces, clasps and cords … Maybe some will say it's too much, but I only say: splendid!

PROJECT SUMMARY

- Cardigan with a hood and two waist cords
- Clasps used for front closure
- The hood has a pompom and tie cord
- The cable pattern has moss stitch at lower edge of body and along the front edges and hood; the sleeves are edged with ribbing
- Worked from the bottom up
- The front, back, and hood are each worked separately, back and forth; the edges in moss stitch are worked at the same time as each front
- The body is worked in the round up to the neck opening, and then worked back and forth; it's then divided at the underarms, and front and back are worked separately, back and forth
- The sleeves are worked back and forth, and are shaped at the underarms with stitches bound off at each side; the remaining stitches are worked to the shoulder as a cap. Once all the pieces are joined, the neckband is worked last

SKILL LEVEL

Experienced

SIZES

38 (40, 42)

FINISHED MEASUREMENTS

Chest: 45 (47¼, 49¾) in / 114 (120, 126) cm
Total Length: 26¾ (27½, 28 ¼) in / 68 (70, 72) cm
Sleeve Length: 18¼ (19, 19¾) in / 46 (48, 50) cm

MATERIALS

Yarn: CYCA #3 (DK, light worsted) Rauma 3-ply Strikkegarn (100% Norwegian wool, 118 yd/108 m / 50 g)

Yarn Colors and Amounts:
White 2001: 950 (1,000, 1,100) g

Needles: U. S. sizes 1.5 and 4 / 2.5 and 3.5 mm: circulars or straights; cable needle

Notions: 7 pewter clasps

GAUGE

22 sts on larger needles = 4 in / 10 cm.
Adjust needle sizes to obtain correct gauge if necessary.

BACK

With larger circular, CO 126 (134, 142) sts. Work back and forth in moss stitch (see chart for Pattern 1) for 1¼ in / 3 cm. On the last row, increase 16 sts evenly spaced across to 142 (150, 158) sts.
Set up pattern sequence as follows: Work 15 (19, 23) moss sts (see chart for Pattern 1), work following chart for Pattern 2, 12 moss sts, switch back to Pattern 2, and moss st over rem 15 (19, 23) sts.
Work in pattern as est until back measures 25 (25¾, 26½) in / 63.5 (65.5, 67.5) cm. BO all sts.

RIGHT FRONT

With larger circular, CO 63 (67, 71) sts. Work back and forth in moss stitch (see chart for Pattern 1) for 1¼ in / 3 cm. On last row, increase 8 sts evenly spaced across to 71 (75, 79) sts.
Set up pattern sequence as follows: Work 6 moss sts (see chart for Pattern 1) for front band, work following chart for Pattern 2, 15 (19, 23) moss sts.
Work in pattern as est until back measures 25 (25¾, 26½) in / 60 (62, 64) cm.
At beginning of every row from band, shape neck: BO 8,4,3,2 sts.
When front measures 25 (25¾, 26½) in / 63.5 (65.5, 67.5) cm, BO all sts.

LEFT FRONT

Work as for right front, but mirror-image.

SLEEVES

With smaller circular, CO 44 (44, 48) sts. Work back and forth in k2, p2 ribbing for 2 in / 5 cm. On last row, increase evenly spaced across to 88 (88, 90) sts.
Change to larger needle. Work Pattern 2 over center 50 sts, and Pattern 1 on each side.
Every ⅝ in / 1.5 cm, increase 1 st at each side a total of 26 (28, 29) times = 140 (144, 148) sts. Work new sts into Pattern 1. Continue in pattern until sleeve measures 18¼ (19, 19⅞) in / 46.5 (48.5, 50.5) cm. BO the outermost 54 (56, 68) sts at each side. Continue in pattern as est but with 3 purl sts at each side.
When sleeve measures 25⅜ (26¾, 28) in / 64.5 (68, 71.5) cm, BO the center 2 sts. BO at front neck: 4 sts 3 times, and 3 sts once. *At the same time*, shape back neck: BO 1 st 2 times, 2 sts 2 times, 2 sts 3 times, and 3 sts once.

HOOD

With larger needles, CO 101 (101, 101) sts. Work back and forth in moss st (see chart for Pattern 1). The center st = center back and is always knitted on all rows; pm on center st. Increase 1 st on each side of center st every ⅝ in / 1.5 cm 28 times. Work new sts into moss st. Continue as est until hood measures 16½ (16½, 16½) in / 42 (42, 42) cm and there are 157 (157, 157) sts. Fold hood and BO towards center with three-needle bind-off or join sts with Kitchener st.
Make a pompom and sew it securely to tip of hood.

FINISHING

Lay pieces flat with a damp towel over them. Leave until completely dry. Attach sleeves to body and then seam sleeves and sides. Seam with WS facing, using back stitch. Sew on hood. Sew on 7 pewter clasps, spaced evenly down front band. Twist 2 cords and thread them through waist of sweater to cinch body. Space each cord about 1¼ in / 3 cm apart. Twist another cord and thread it through edging of hood.
Gently steam press garment under a damp pressing cloth.

Pattern 1 (moss stitch)

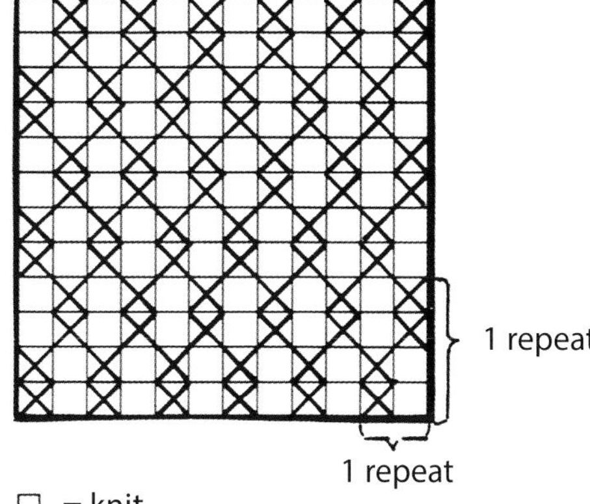

□ = knit
⊠ = purl

Pattern 2

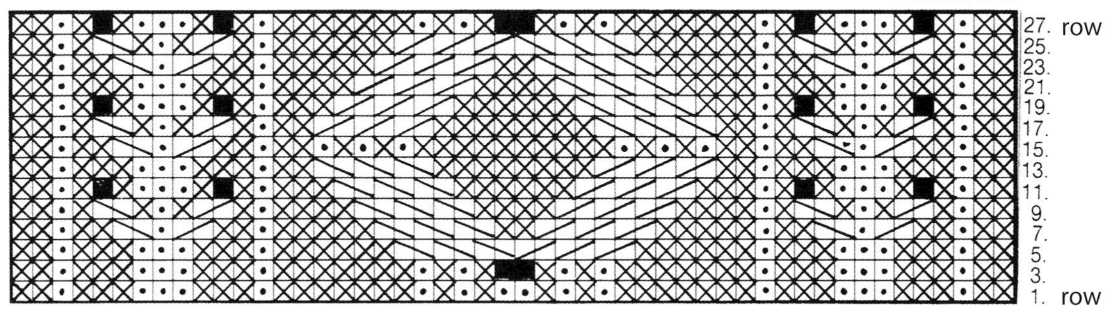

Note: Rows 1-4 are only worked at lower edge.
Rows 5-28 are repeated.

The chart shows only RS rows.
On WS rows (Rows 2, 4, 6, etc), knit all knit sts and purl all purl sts, and work all twisted sts as twisted.

⊡ = twisted knit

⊠ = purl

[/] = place 1 st on cable needle and hold in back of work, k1tbl, p1 from cable needle.

[\] = place 1 st on cable needle and hold in front of work, p1, k1tbl from cable needle.

■ = knot: work 5 sts into 1 st: (k1, p1, k1, p1, k1) into same st; turn. K5 tbl; turn. K2tog, k3tog and pass first st over second.

■■ = large knot over 2 sts: K1, yo twice, k1; turn, p1, work yarnovers as k1tbl, p1; turn. P4; turn. K2tog, k2tog.

Small and Cozy

Sometimes, smaller knitting projects are delightful—the ones that don't take too much time, and are easy to carry along in your bag. These select small garments are, in addition, cozy and good for pulling over cold ears, hands, or feet.

Spotted Socks

If you want to make a point, you can do it—many times—with yarn and knitting needles. These spotted socks will make a lasting point.

Design: Rauma Garn / Britt Kathrine Aasen
Photos: Pudder Agency / Julie Pike

PROJECT SUMMARY

- The same pattern—different color combinations
- Worked from the top down
- Stockinette with ribbing for the cuff
- Heel as continuation of leg

SKILL LEVEL

Experienced

SIZES

Women's (Men's)

FINISHED MEASUREMENTS

Foot Length: approx. 9½ (10¾) in / 24 (27) cm

MATERIALS

Yarn: CYCA # 1 (fingering) Rauma 2-ply Gammelserie (100% Norwegian wool, 175 yd/160 m / 50 g)

Yarn Colors and Amounts:

Petroleum GL4902 or Burgundy GL4901: 50 (100) g
Ochre Yellow GL4905 or Mustard Yellow GL4805: 50 (50) g
Natural GL401: 50 (50) g

Needles: U. S. sizes 0 and 1.5 / 2 and 2.5 mm: sets of 5 dpn

GAUGE

28 sts in stockinette pattern on larger needles = 4 in / 10 cm in width.
Adjust needle sizes to obtain correct gauge if necessary.
NOTE: If you work more tightly in two-color stranded knitting than in a single color, go up a needle size for the colorwork.

KNITTING TIPS

* For more durable socks, you can hold a fine yarn together with 2-ply Gammelserie for heels and toes. The best reinforcement yarns have some nylon.
* To avoid holes on the heel shaping, try this: Pick up the strand between stitches. On the next round, work the last stitch before turning and then passthe last stitch over the extra stitch.

SOCK

With Yellow and smaller dpn, CO 58 (64) sts. Divide sts onto dpn and join. Work around in k1, p1 ribbing for 1½ in / 4 cm. Change to larger dpn. Knit 1 rnd, *at the same time* increasing to 60 (66) sts. Now work leg following chart for Pattern A until sock measures approx. 7 (8) / 18 (20) cm, ending with either Row 1 or Row 7 of chart. Work heel back and forth.

HEEL

See Knitting Tips above. With Yellow, work heel over the first and last 14 (16) sts of rnd = 28 (32 sts). Begin on RS and work back and forth in stockinette. Shape heel as follows: Work all sts; turn and work 27 (31) sts. Turn and work 26 (30) sts. Turn and work 1 less st than

on previous row for each turn until 8 sts rem at center of heel. On next and following rows, work 1 more st for each turn until you once again work across all heel sts.

FOOT

Work in the round over all sts. Continue in pattern until foot measures approx. 8 (8¾) in / 20 (22) cm or desired length before toe (allow approx. 2 in / 5 cm for length of toe). End pattern with row marked on chart.

TOE

See Knitting Tips at beginning of pattern. With Yellow, shape toe: [K2tog, k8 (9)] around. Knit 1 rnd without decreasing.

[K2tog, k7 (8)] around. Knit 1 rnd without decreasing. Rep last 2 rnds, with 1 st less between decreases each decrease rnd.

Last Rnd: K2tog around.

FINISHING

Cut yarn. Draw end through rem sts and tighten. Weave in all ends neatly on WS.

Make second sock the same way.

Pattern A

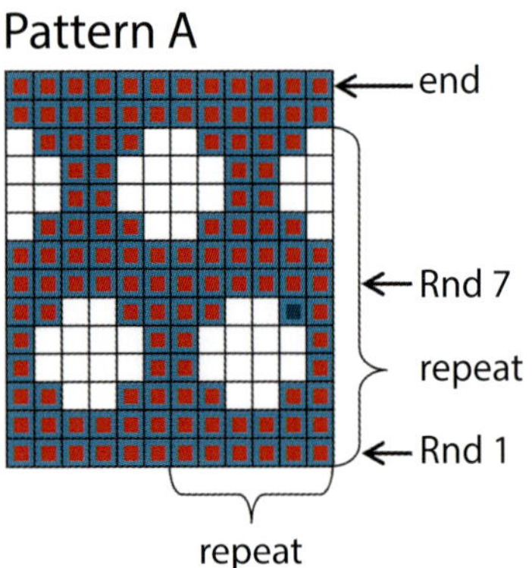

☐ Natural

■ Petroleum or Burgundy

Fitted Felted Mittens

I think it feels a little like Christmas when I take a newly felted pair of wool mittens out of the washing machine. Is what I have in my hands something useful? Will they fit? It's just as exciting every time! These mittens are so delightful to wear and are just the right size.

Design: Rauma Garn / Ane Tyssøy Godal
Photos: Siren Lauvdal

PROJECT SUMMARY

- Worked from the top down
- Stockinette
- Shaped with a thumb gusset
- Felted in the washing machine

SKILL LEVEL

Easy/Intermediate

SIZES

3-5 years (7-9 years, 11-14 years, Women's, Men's)

FINISHED MEASUREMENTS

Circumference: 7 (8, 8¾, 8¾, 9¾) in / 18 (20, 22, 22, 25) cm
Length: approx. 8 (8¾, 9¾, 11, 11½) in / 20 (22, 25, 28, 29) cm

MATERIALS

Yarn: CYCA #5 (bulky) Rauma Vams PT3 (100% Norwegian wool, 90 yd/83 m / 50 g)

Yarn Colors and Amounts:
Light Heather Yellow V304 or Moss Green V406 or Light Rose V302: 100 (100, 100, 100, 150) g

Needles: U. S. size 8 / 5 mm: set of 5 dpn

GAUGE

16 sts in stockinette, after felting = 4 in / 10 cm in width.
Adjust needle sizes to obtain correct gauge if necessary.

RIGHT MITTEN

CO 28 (30, 34, 34, 40) sts. Divide sts onto dpn and join.
Purl 1 rnd and then work in stockinette (knit all rnds) for 3¼ (4, 4¼, 4¾, 6) in / 8 (10, 11, 12, 15) cm. On next rnd, increase for thumb gusset:
Gusset Increase Rnd: K1 (2, 2, 3, 3), yo, k1, yo, knit to end of rnd.
On next rnd, work all yarnovers as k1tbl.
K3 (4, 5, 5, 6, 6) rnds.
Gusset Rnd 2: K2 (2, 2, 1, 1), place next 4 (5, 6, 7, 8) sts on a holder for thumb, knit to end of rnd.
Next Rnd: Over thumbhole gap, CO 2 (3, 4, 5, 6) sts.
Continue knitting around until mitten covers top of index finger or measures 2¾ (3½, 4¼, 4¾, 5½) in / 7 (9, 11, 12, 14) cm above thumbhole. Pm on each side with 14 (15, 17, 17, 20) sts on each side.
Shape top as follows: (Knit until 2 sts before marker, sl 1, k2tog, psso) 2 times = 4 sts decreased around. Decrease the same way on every other rnd until 4 (6, 6, 6, 8) sts rem.
Cut yarn. Draw end through rem sts and tighten.

LEFT MITTEN

Work as for right mitten, but place thumbhole on opposite side: Increase for thumb gusset after 12 (12, 14, 13, 16) sts and place sts on holder after 10 (10, 11, 11, 13) sts.

THUMB

Divide held thumb sts onto dpn and pick up and knit 2 (3, 4, 5, 6) sts over cast-on sts + 1 new st at each side of thumbhole = 8 (10, 12, 14, 16) sts total. Work around in stockinette for 1½ (2, 2½, 2¾, 3¼) in / 4 (5, 6, 7, 8) cm. Shape top of thumb as for top of mitten hand, decreasing until 4 (6, 4, 6, 4) sts rem. Cut yarn. Draw end through rem sts and tighten.

Weave in all ends neatly on WS.

FELTING

Felt mittens in the washing machine at 104°F / 40°C, short program, for approx. 1 hour, with gentle spinning. Use a liquid wool-safe soap (the mittens can also be felted without any soap). If you are only felting one pair of mittens, add a towel to the wash. While mittens are still damp, stretch into correct shape and size; measure and lay flat until completely dry.

Happy Shawl

So lovely to have a nice large scarf to wrap around yourself on a cool evening … or on a chilly day, if you're a little shivery. You can knit it in whatever fine yarn you like, and the shawl will have a different thickness or size depending on the yarn you choose.

Design: Rauma Garn / Marie Cecilie Dahl
Photos: Janne Rugland

PROJECT SUMMARY

- Rectangular shawl
- Lace pattern surrounded by garter stitch edges and a pattern that looks just as nice on both sides
- Can easily be knitted in other types or weights of yarn

SKILL LEVEL

Intermediate/Experienced

FINISHED MEASUREMENTS

Lamullgarn: 21 x 57 in / 53 x 145 cm
Finullgarn: 23¾ x 57 in / 60 x 145 cm

MATERIALS

Yarn:
CYCA #1 (light fingering) Rauma Lamullgarn (100% Norwegian wool, 273 yd/250 m / 50 g)
OR
CYCA #2 (sport, baby) Rauma Finull (100% Norwegian wool, 191 yd/175 m / 50 g)

Yarn Colors and Amounts:
Lamullgarn: Natural L11: 300 g
Finullgarn: Khaki Green 489: 400 g

Needles:
Lamullgarn: U. S. size 2.5 / 3 mm: circular
Finullgarn: U. S. size 4 / 3.5 mm: circular

GAUGE

Lamullgarn: 29 sts in lace pattern = 4 in / 10 cm in width.
Finullgarn: 26 sts in lace pattern = 4 in / 10 cm in width.
Adjust needle sizes to obtain correct gauge if necessary.

SHAWL

CO 155 sts. Work back and forth. Knit 6 rows = 3 ridges; the first row = WS.
NOTE: Always slip the first st throughout for a neat edge.
After garter edge, work in Pattern A until piece measures 56¾ in / 144 cm or desired length.
Knit 6 rows and then BO.

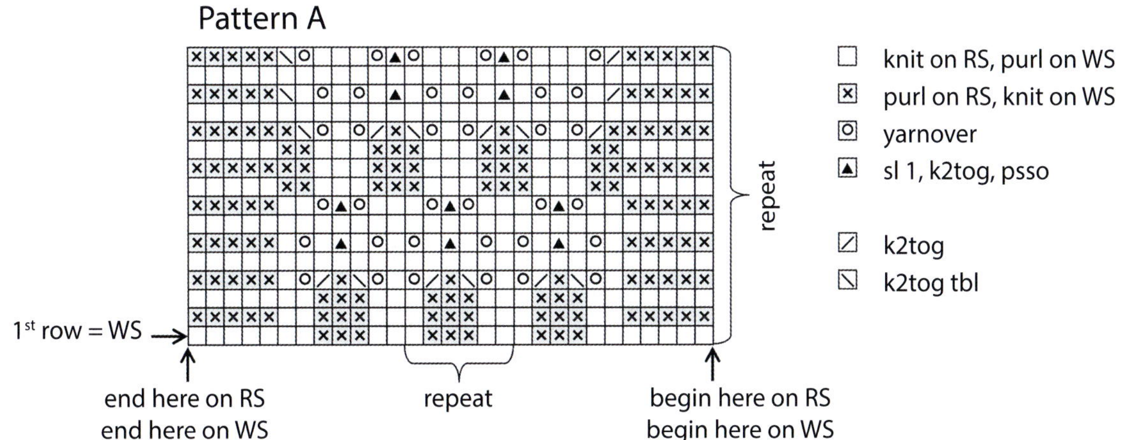

Zigzag Slippers

Cold floors? In that case, these slippers are a "must" for keeping your toes warm. We've suggested two different types of yarn for these slippers—the yarn choice and your gauge will determine the finished size.

Design: Rauma Garn / Britt Kathrine Aasen
Photos: Hilde Kvivik Kavli

PROJECT SUMMARY

- Stockinette in two-color stranded knitting pattern
- Size is determined by gauge
- Worked toe up
- The placement of the heel in marked by a row worked in scrap yarn; later, the scrap yarn is removed and the heel is worked over the r eleased stitches

SKILL LEVEL

Experienced

SIZES

Women's (Men's)

FINISHED MEASUREMENTS

Foot Length: approx. 8¾ (10¼) in / 22 (26) cm

MATERIALS

Yarn:

Women's: CYCA #1 (fingering) Rauma 2-ply Gammelserie (100% Norwegian wool, 175 yd/160 m / 50 g)
Men's: CYCA #3 (DK, light worsted) Rauma 3-ply Strikkegarn (100% Norwegian wool, 118 yd/108 m / 50 g)

Yarn Colors and Amounts:
Women's with Gammelserie:
Peasant Blue GL438: 50 g
Natural GL401: 50 g

Men's with Strikkegarn:
Peasant Blue 138: 100 g
Natural 101: 50 g

Needles:
Women's: U. S. size 2.5 / 3 mm: set of 5 dpn
Men's: U. S. size 4 / 3.5 mm: set of 5 dpn

GAUGE

Women's: 26 sts and 32 rnds in stockinette pattern with Gammelserie and needles U. S. 2.5 / 3 mm = 4 x 4 in / 10 x 10 cm.
Men's: 24 sts and 28 rnds in stockinette pattern with Strikkegarn and needles U. S. 4 / 3.5 mm = 4 x 4 in / 10 x 10 cm.
Adjust needle sizes to obtain correct gauge if necessary.
NOTE: If you knit more tightly in two-color stranded knitting than in a single color, go up a needle size for the colorwork.

SLIPPERS

With Peasant Blue and dpn, CO 10 sts, Work 15 rows back and forth in stockinette = toe. Pick up and knit 14 sts on each side of toe (= a and b on Pattern A), and 10 sts in cast-on row = 48 sts. Divide sts onto 4 dpn and join. Work around in Pattern A, increasing as shown on chart. At the red line on the chart, knit 35 sts with a smooth scrap yarn. Continue in pattern until chart is complete and then work 6 rnds in stockinette with Peasant Blue. BO loosely.

HEEL

Insert one dpn through sts below scrap yarn and another in sts above scrap yarn. Carefully remove scrap yarn and divide the 70 sts onto 4 dpn. Increase 1 st at each side. Work Pattern B, decreasing as shown on chart:

At beginning of Ndls 1 and 3, sl 1, k1, psso.

At end of Ndls 2 and 4, k2tog.

After chart for Pattern B is finished, 20 sts rem. Join the two sets of 10 sts with Kitchener st or 3-needle bind-off. Weave in all ends neatly on WS.

Make the second slipper to match, reversing shaping and pattern to correspond.

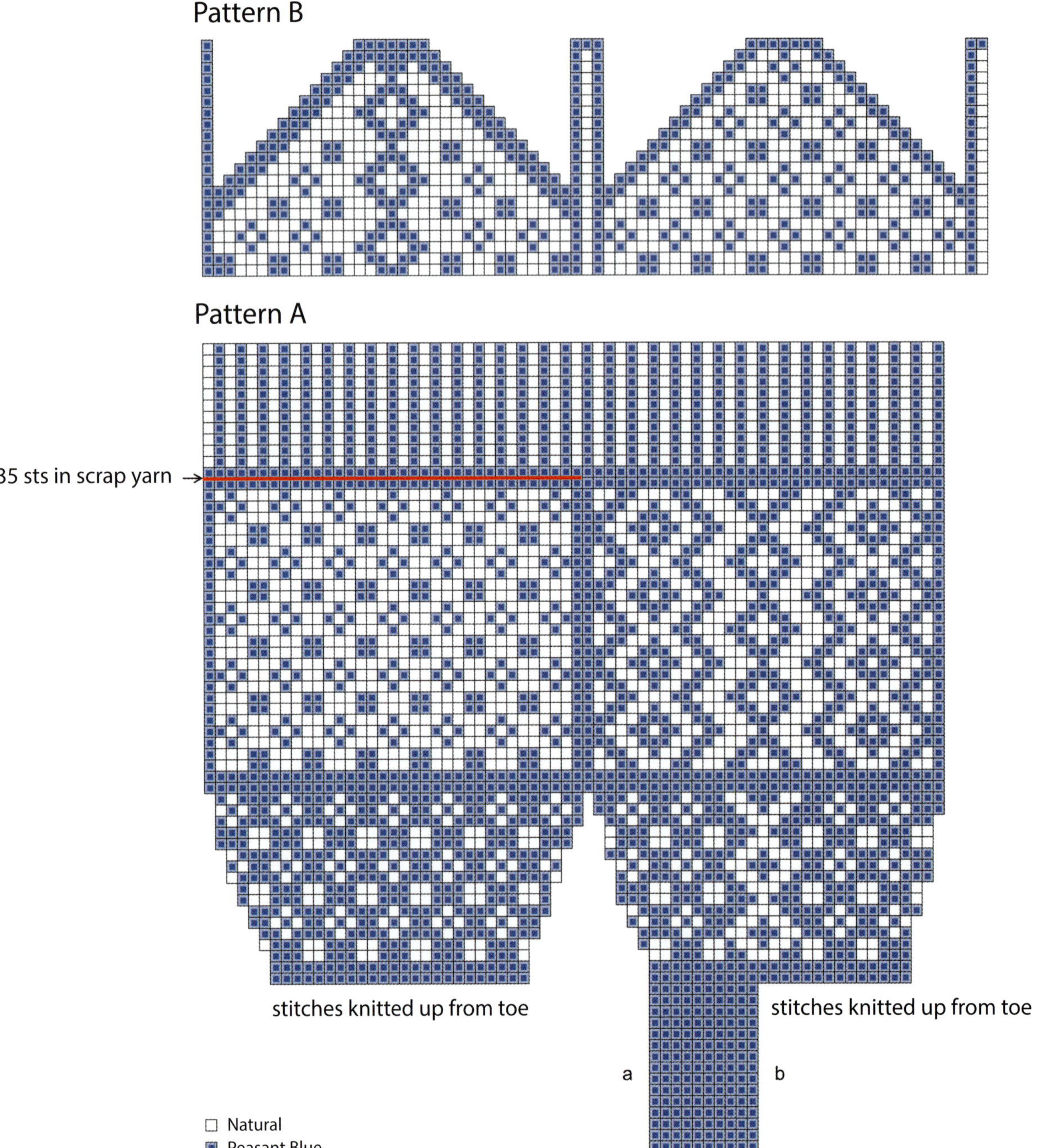

"Quick-Knit" Hat and "Fast-Finish" Scarf

As you may have noticed, when your yarn is thick, you can see the knitted garment grow with every stitch you make. It's certainly true with this hat and scarf ensemble—these projects will work up really fast! And in a delightful combo of cables and seed stitch.

Design: Rauma Garn / Camilla Dingsøyr Lôkal Oslo
Photos: Siren Lauvdal

PROJECT SUMMARY

- Hat and scarf both worked with yarn held double
- Both pieces worked with cables and seed stitch; the hat has a ribbed brim

HAT

SKILL LEVEL

Intermediate/Experienced

SIZES

XS/S (M/L)

FINISHED MEASUREMENTS

Head Circumference: 19-21¾ (21-22¾) in / 48-55 (53-58) cm
Length: 9 (9½) in / 23 (24) cm

MATERIALS

Yarn: CYCA #5 (bulky) Rauma Vams PT3 (100% Norwegian wool, 90 yd/83 m / 50 g)

Yarn Colors and Amounts:
Red V24 or Midnight Blue V77: 100 (100) g

Needles: U. S. size 15 / 10 mm: short circular; cable needle

GAUGE

9 sts in seed st with yarn held double = 4 in / 10 cm in width.
Adjust needle size to obtain correct gauge if necessary.

DECREASE TIPS

Decreasing before a marker = k2tog: knit or purl depending on how st to right should be worked in pattern.
Decreasing after a marker = k2tog: knit or purl depending on how st to left should be worked in pattern.

HAT

Holding two strands of yarn together, CO 44 (48) sts. Join, being careful not to twist cast-on row; pm for beginning of rnd. Work 10 rnds k1, p1 ribbing and then work following chart for Pattern A. On the rnd before the first decrease rnd, pm at the sides as follows: Work 10 (12) sts, pm, work 24 (24) sts, pm, work to end of rnd. On all decrease rnds marked in pattern, work 2 sts tog on each side of markers (see Decrease Tips above) = 4 sts decreased around. End at arrow for your size. On next rnd, k2tog around, binding off at the same time.

FINISHING

Seam hat at top.

Pattern A

last rnd M/L

last rnd XS/S

4th decrease rnd

3rd decrease rnd

2nd decrease rnd

1st decrease rnd

begin

work 8 (9) times | cable (12 sts) | work 8 (9) times

knit

purl

place 2 sts on a cable needle and hold in back of work, k2, k2 from cable needle

place 2 sts on a cable needle and hold in front of work, k2, k2 from cable needle

place 3 sts on a cable needle and hold in back of work, k3, k3 from cable needle

place 3 sts on a cable needle and hold in front of work, k3, k3 from cable needle

SCARF

SKILL LEVEL

Intermediate/Experienced

FINISHED MEASUREMENTS

Width: approx. 13¾ in / 35 cm

Length: approx. 78¾ in / 200 cm

MATERIALS

Yarn: CYCA #5 (bulky) Rauma Vams PT3 (100% Norwegian wool, 90 yd/83 m / 50 g)

Yarn Colors and Amounts:

Red V24 or Midnight Blue V77: 600 g

Needles: U. S. size 15 / 10 mm: short circular; cable needle

GAUGE

9 sts in seed st with yarn held double = 4 in / 10 cm in width.

Adjust needle size to obtain correct gauge if necessary.

SCARF

Holding two strands of yarn together, CO 42 sts. Work back and forth in Pattern B until scarf measures approx. 76¾ in / 195 cm or desired length. End with 8 rows after last cable crossing, as shown on chart. BO.

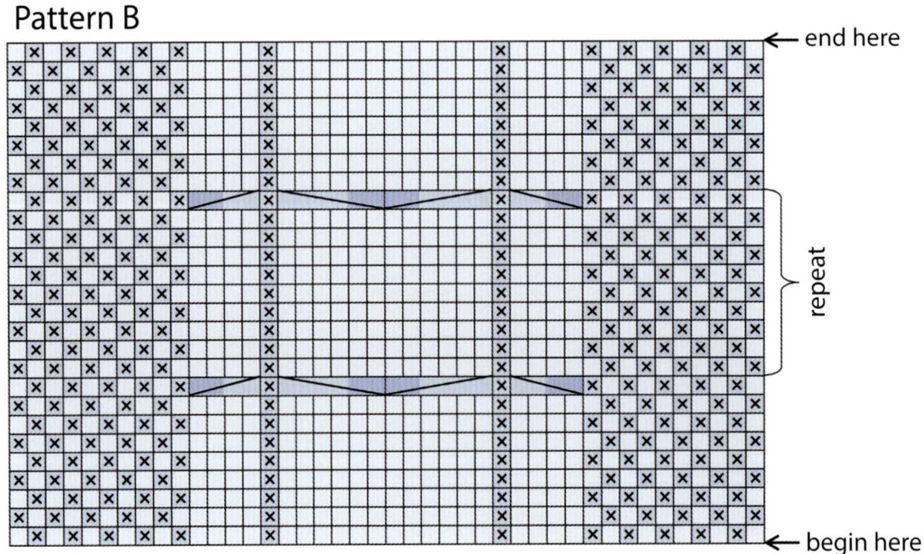

GEMS FROM THE ARCHIVE

Mittens from Manndalen

Manndalen is a town in the municipality of Kåjord, in Troms and Finnmark (in northern Norway). The town has a population of about a thousand. *(Source: Wikipedia)*

Mittens from Manndalen were traditionally knitted in white and black, and then embroidered with duplicate stitch to fill in the colored sections. The color choices and smaller embroidered details varied from maker to maker. (*Source: manndalen-husflidslag.no)*

PROJECT SUMMARY

- Worked from the cuff up
- Stockinette in two-color pattern with ribbing at the top.
- Increases for thumb gusset
- The mittens are finished with pattern colors embroidered using duplicate stitch

Mittens from Manndalen

SKILL LEVEL

Experienced

SIZES

3-6 years (7-10 years, 11-14 years, Women's, Men's)

MATERIALS

Yarn: CYCA # 3 (DK, light worsted) Rauma 3-ply Strikkegarn (100% Norwegian wool, 118 yd/108 m / 50 g)

Yarn Colors and Amounts:

□ MC: White 101: 50 (50, 50, 100, 100) g

☒ CC: Black 136: 50 (50, 50, 100, 100) g

⊡ Small amounts in a variety of colors, for example Red 174, Blue 167, Yellow 131, Green 123 (will be worked later in duplicate stitch)

Needles: U. S. size 1.5 and 2.5 / 2.5 and 3 mm: sets of 5 dpn

GAUGE

24 sts in stockinette pattern = 4 in / 10 cm.
Adjust needle sizes to obtain correct gauge if necessary.

MITTEN

With MC and smaller dpn, CO 32 (36, 40, 48, 52) sts. Divide sts onto 4 dpn and join. Work around in k2, p2 ribbing for 7 (9, 10, 12, 12) rnds. With CC, work 1 rnd; work 2 rnds MC, 3 rnds CC, 2 rnds MC, 1 rnd CC, and 7 (9, 10, 12, 12) rnds with MC.

Change to larger dpn. Knit 1 rnd, increasing evenly spaced around to 34 (38, 42, 50, 54) sts. Work following chart for pattern for chosen size. A ⊡ on chart is knitted with MC (White), and then pattern colors are added later with duplicate stitch.

Increase for the thumb gusset as shown on chart.

At A on chart, place 9 (9, 9, 11, 11) sts on holder for thumb. On next rnd, CO 9 (9, 9, 11, 11) sts over gap.

Continue following chart, decreasing as shown:

At beginning of Ndls 1 and 3: Work side st, sl 1, k1, psso.

At end of Ndls 2 and 4: K2tog.

Decrease until 8 (8, 8, 6, 6) sts rem.

Cut yarn and draw end through rem sts; tighten.

Thumb 7-10 years:

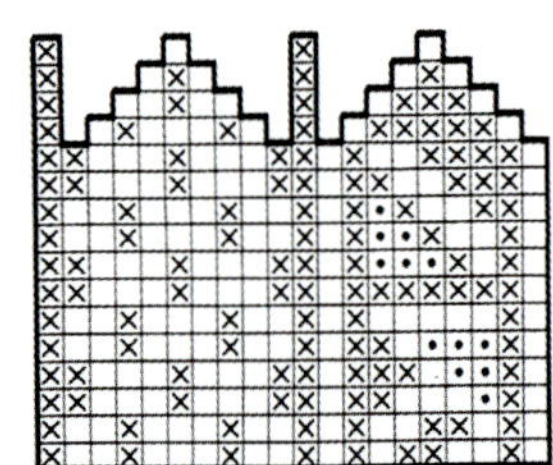

THUMB

Move held thumb sts to larger dpn. On underside of thumb, pick up and knit 1 (1, 2, 1, 2) sts at each side. Work following chart for pattern and decrease as shown. Cut yarn and draw end through rem sts; tighten.

Make second mitten the same way, reversing shaping—make sure thumb is on opposite side of palm.

Use duplicate stitch to fill in color sections (see photo for example).

Mittens 3-6 years:

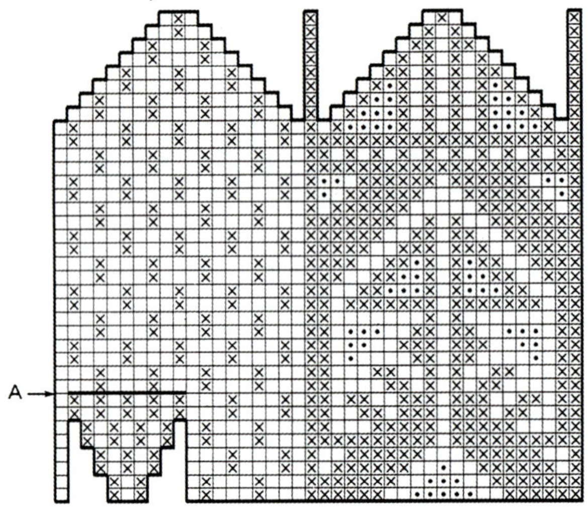

Thumb 3-6 years:

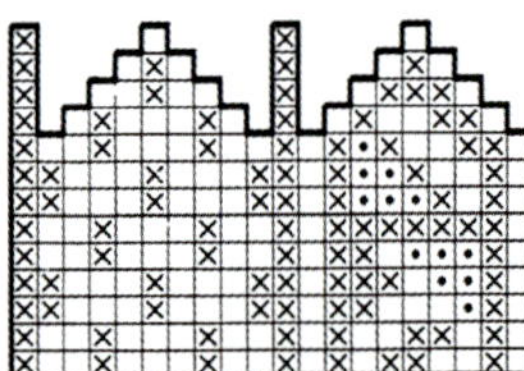

Mittens 7-10 years:

Mittens 11-14 years:

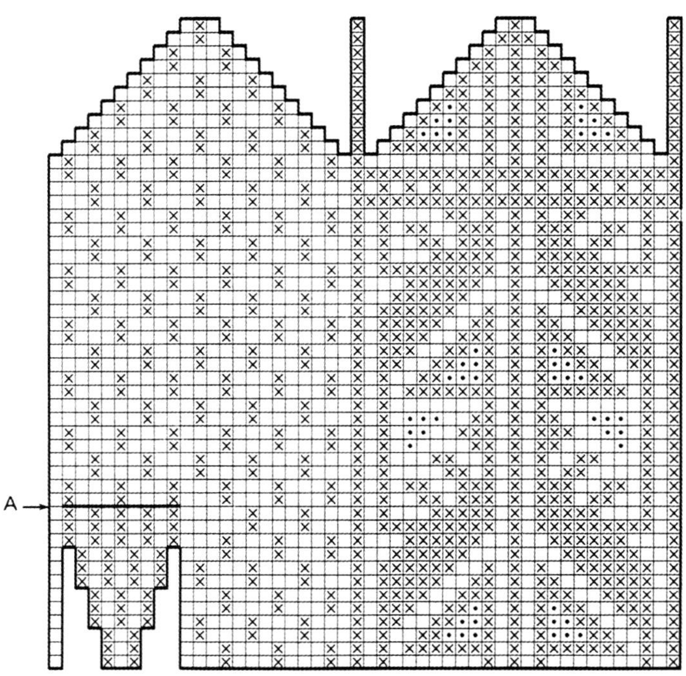

Thumb 11-14 years:

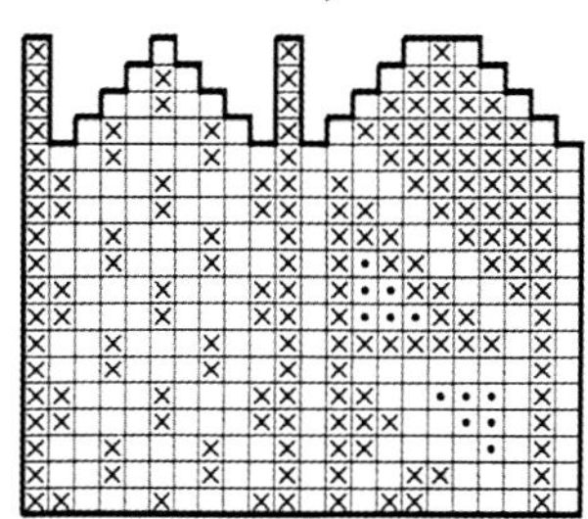

Women's Mittens:

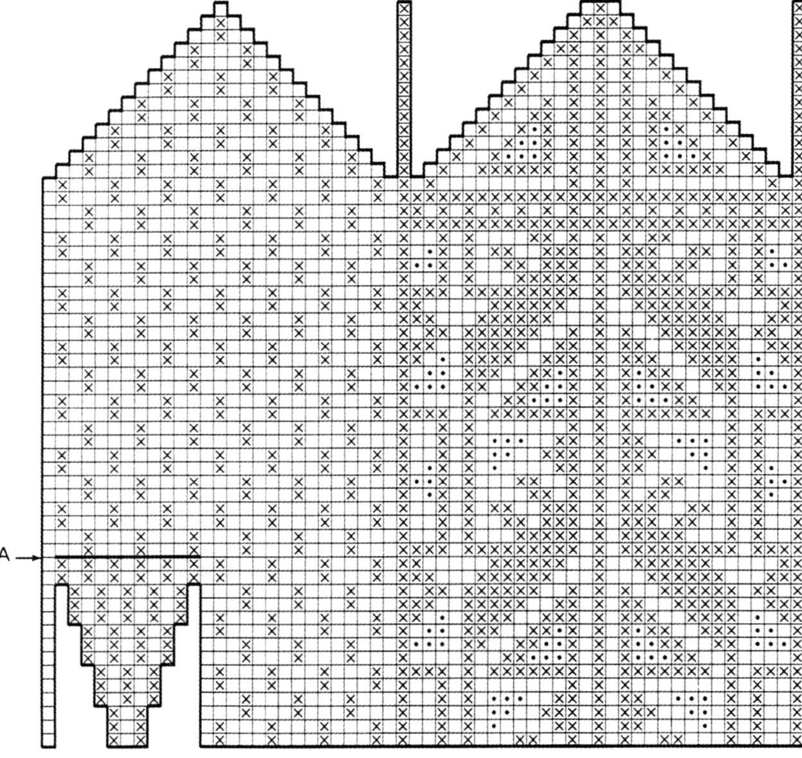

Thumb Women's Mittens:

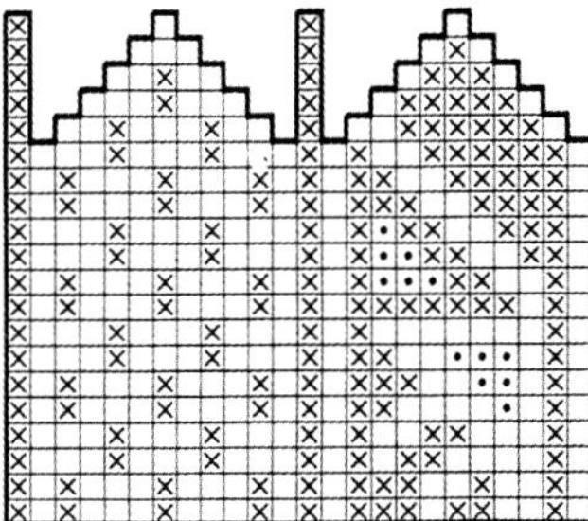

Men's Mittens:

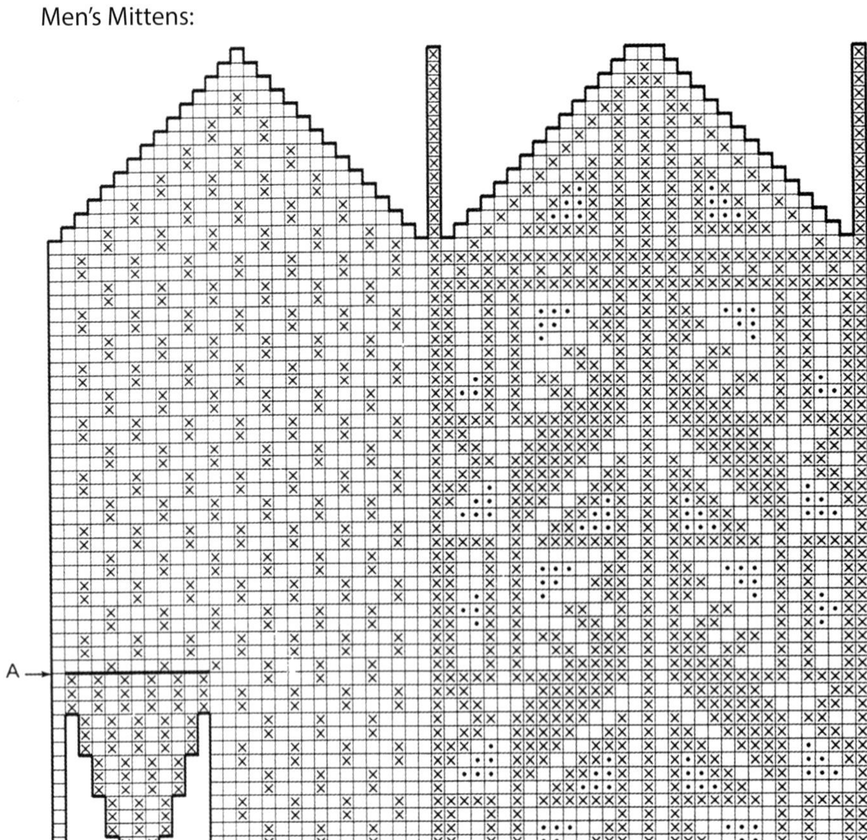

Thumb Men's Mittens:

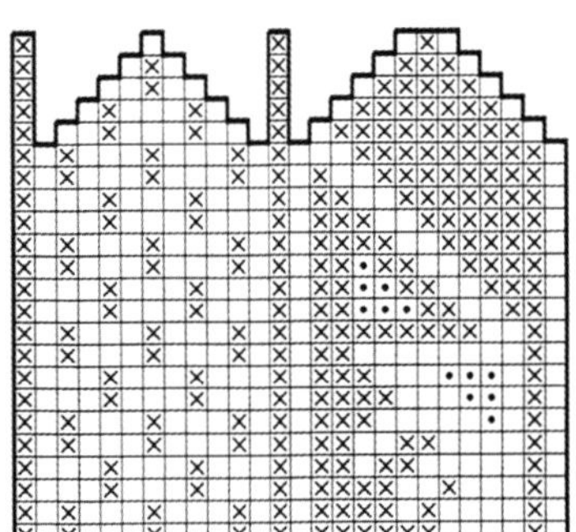

Duplicate stitch:

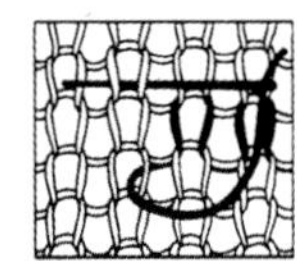

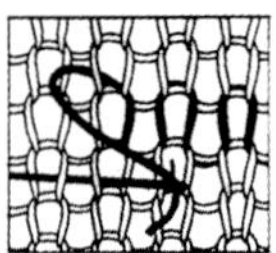

Finally

ABBREVIATIONS

BO	bind off (= UK cast off)
CC	contrast (pattern) color
cm	centimeters
CO	cast on
dpn	double-pointed needles
in	inch(es)
g	grams
k	knit
k2tog	knit 2 together (= 1 stitch decreased; right-leaning decrease)
k3tog	knit 3 together (= 2 stitches decreased; right-leaning decrease)
m	meters
MC	main (background) color
mm	millimeters
p	purl
p2tog	purl 2 together (= 1 stitch decreased)
pm	place marker
psso	pass slipped stitch over
rem	remain(s)(ing)
rep	repeat
RS	right side
sl	slip
sl m	slip marker
st(s)	stitch(es)
tbl	through back loop(s)
tog	together
WS	wrong side
wyb	with yarn held in back
wyf	with yarn held in front
yd	yard(s)
yo	yarnover

steek A steek is a section of extra stitches added so that you can knit in the round on a sweater body that will later be cut open for the two fronts of a cardigan or for the armholes from underarms to shoulders, or for the neck (for example, a placket). Instructions for working the steek stitches and for reinforcing and cutting a steek are given in individual patterns. Usually the steek stitches are worked in alternating pattern colors or with one color for single-color row.

YARN INFORMATION

Rauma yarns are available from:
The Yarn Guys
theyarnguys.com

The Woolly Thistle
thewoollythistle.com

Some specific yarn types or weights may be difficult to find. A variety of additional and substitute yarns are available from:
Webs—America's Yarn Store
75 Service Center Road
Northampton, MA 01060
800-367-9327
yarn.com

LoveKnitting.com
loveknitting.com/us

If you are unable to obtain any of the yarn used in this book, it can be replaced with a yarn of a similar weight and composition. Please note, however, the finished projects may vary slightly from those shown, depending on the yarn used. Try www.yarnsub.com for suggestions.

For more information on selecting or substituting yarn, contact your local yarn shop or an online store; they are familiar with all types of yarns and would be happy to help you. Additionally, the online knitting community at Ravelry.com has forums where you can post questions about specific yarns. Yarns come and go so quickly these days and there are so many beautiful yarns available.